NELSON

IMPACT™

Bible Study Series

D1195850

PARABLES
OF JESUS

Mark

NELSON IMPACT

A Division of Thomas Nelson Publishers

Since 1798

www.thomasnelson.com

Published by Nelson Impact, a Division of Thomas Nelson, Inc., P.O. Box 141000, Nashville, Tennessee, 37214.

Scripture quotations marked NKJV are taken from the *The Holy Bible,* The New King James Version®. Copyright © 1979, 1980, 1982, 1992 Thomas Nelson, Inc., Publishers.

ISBN 1-4185-0618-4

Printed in the United States of America.

06 07 08 EB 9 8 7 6 5 4 3 2 1

A Word from the Publisher...

Be diligent to present yourself approved to God, a worker who does not need to be ashamed, rightly dividing the word of truth.

2 Timothy 2:15 NKJV

We are so glad that you have chosen this study guide to enrich your biblical knowledge and strengthen your walk with God. Inside you will find great information that will deepen your understanding and knowledge of this book of the Bible.

Many tools are included to aid you in your study, including ancient and present-day maps of the Middle East, as well as timelines and charts to help you understand when the book was written and why. You will also benefit from sidebars placed strategically throughout this study guide, designed to give you expanded knowledge of language, theology, culture, and other details regarding the Scripture being studied.

We consider it a joy and a ministry to serve you and teach you through these study guides. May your heart be blessed, your mind expanded, and your spirit lifted as you walk through God's Word.

Blessings,

Edward (Les) Middleton, M.Div.
Editor-in-Chief, Nelson Impact

TIMELINE OF NEW

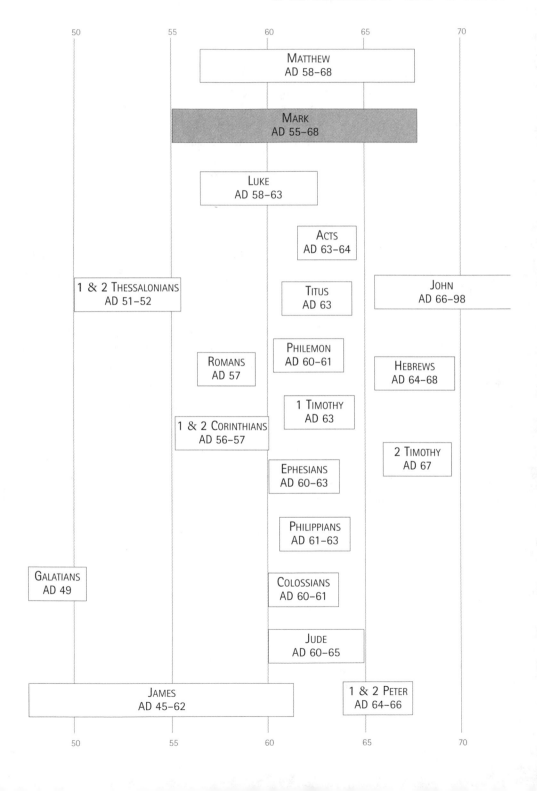

50	55	60	65	70

MATTHEW AD 58–68

MARK AD 55–68

LUKE AD 58–63

ACTS AD 63–64

1 & 2 THESSALONIANS AD 51–52

TITUS AD 63

JOHN AD 66–98

PHILEMON AD 60–61

ROMANS AD 57

HEBREWS AD 64–68

1 TIMOTHY AD 63

1 & 2 CORINTHIANS AD 56–57

2 TIMOTHY AD 67

EPHESIANS AD 60–63

PHILIPPIANS AD 61–63

GALATIANS AD 49

COLOSSIANS AD 60–61

JUDE AD 60–65

JAMES AD 45–62

1 & 2 PETER AD 64–66

50	55	60	65	70

TESTAMENT WRITINGS

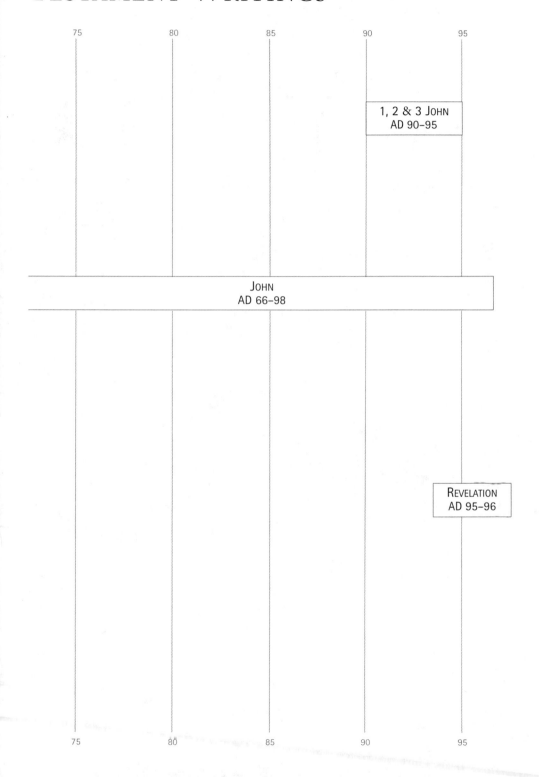

75   80   85   90   95

1, 2 & 3 JOHN
AD 90–95

JOHN
AD 66–98

REVELATION
AD 95–96

75   80   85   90   95

OLD MIDDLE EAST

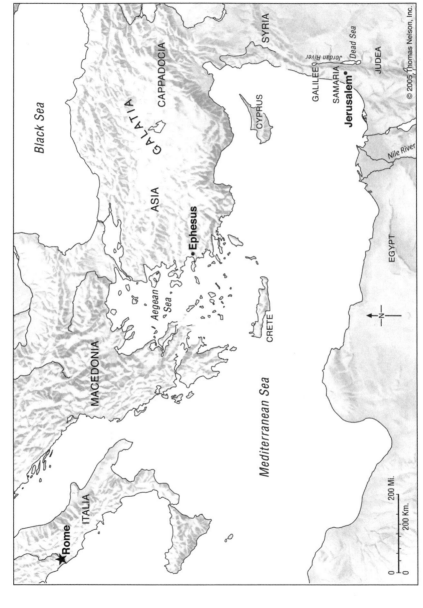

★ Most scholars agree that the book of Mark was written in Rome.

MIDDLE EAST OF TODAY

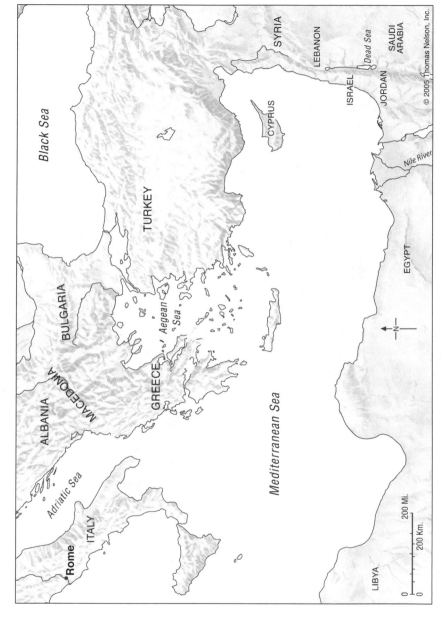

OLD TESTAMENT DIVISIONS

The Pentateuch
Genesis
Exodus
Leviticus
Numbers
Deuteronomy

Wisdom Literature
Job
Psalms
Proverbs
Ecclesiastes
Song of Solomon

The Historical Books
Joshua
Judges
Ruth
1 Samuel
2 Samuel
1 Kings
2 Kings
1 Chronicles
2 Chronicles
Ezra
Nehemiah
Esther

The Prophetic Books
Isaiah
Jeremiah
Lamentations
Ezekiel
Daniel
Hosea
Joel
Amos
Obadiah
Jonah
Micah
Nahum
Habakkuk
Zephaniah
Haggai
Zechariah
Malachi

New Testament Divisions

The Four Gospels
Matthew
Mark
Luke
John

History
Acts

The Epistles of Paul
Romans
1 Corinthians
2 Corinthians
Galatians
Ephesians
Philippians
Colossians
1 Thessalonians
2 Thessalonians
1 Timothy
2 Timothy
Titus
Philemon

The General Epistles
Hebrews
James
1 Peter
2 Peter
1 John
2 John
3 John
Jude

Apocalyptic Literature
Revelation

ICON KEY

Throughout this study guide, you will find many icon sidebars that will aid and enrich your study of this book of the Bible. To help you identify what these icons represent, please refer to the key below.

BIBLICAL GRAB BAG

A biblical grab bag full of interesting facts and tidbits.

BIBLE

Further exploration of biblical principles and interpretations, along with a little food for thought.

LANGUAGE

Word usages, definitions, interpretations, and information on the Greek and Hebrew languages.

CULTURE

Customs, traditions, and lifestyle practices in biblical times.

ARCHAEOLOGICAL

Archaeological discoveries and artifacts that relate to biblical life, as well as modern-day discoveries.

CONTENTS

Introduction

For the reader who is learning about Jesus Christ for the first time, the Gospel of Mark may be the ideal introduction. It is the shortest of the four Gospels, told in a journalistic, action-packed style reminiscent of an eyewitness report. Despite its brevity, it is filled with colorful details, including unforgettable emotional responses by Jesus and those around him. No wonder that on new mission fields, Mark is often the first book translated into the native language. If other books of the Bible can be likened to movie documentaries, then Mark may best resemble a gripping, fast-paced thriller.

The Gospel of Mark is unique in that it does not focus on the genealogy or teachings of Jesus. Instead, it is primarily a record of Jesus' actions and achievements—what He did more than what He said. Eighteen of Christ's miracles are related in Mark, compared to only four of His parables. Through these miracles, and most powerfully through His resurrection, Jesus is unmistakably revealed as the mighty Son of God sent to save the world.

At the same time, Mark places great emphasis on a humbler aspect of Jesus' ministry, His role as God's perfect servant. This Gospel is the story of One who put aside any outward evidence of His glory in heaven in order to assume the form of a servant on earth. Jesus' every word and deed was in obedience to His Father's will. He is portrayed as someone who "did not come to be served, but to serve, and to give His life a ransom for many" (Mark 10:45 NKJV).

The author of Mark most likely identified closely with Jesus' mission as a servant. Mark himself was a "servant," or attendant, of the apostle Paul, and then of his cousin Barnabas. According to most accounts, he was also an attendant of Peter during the final years before the apostle's death. He was ideally suited to write about God's perfect servant.

A LIFE OF SERVICE

The Gospels do not name their authors, so it is impossible to prove conclusively who is responsible for Mark. The title "according to Mark" was added by a scribe sometime before AD 125. But nearly all scholars today accept the unanimous testimony of the early church fathers that Mark was the author. One of these was a man named Papias, a bishop in the early church, who sometime around AD 110 quoted "John the Elder" (thought to be the apostle John) as identifying Mark as the author.

Mark was a Jewish Christian, the son of Mary of Jerusalem. Mary owned a house there that Christians of the early church used as a meeting place. Because Mark includes several details that the other Gospels do not, some have suggested that Mark's home was the site of Jesus' Last Supper before His crucifixion—if true, that was certainly a great honor!

As a youth, Mark likely knew Peter and other early church leaders. As an adult, he accompanied Paul and Barnabas on their first missionary journey, but left in the middle of this journey to return home. No one today knows the reason for Mark's departure, but it apparently caused a falling-out with Paul, as he refused to take Mark on his second journey. Instead, Mark continued to serve with Barnabas on the island of Cyprus. Later, though, Mark regained Paul's confidence. He was a fellow worker when Paul was first imprisoned in Rome. After Paul's release, Mark stayed on in Rome and assisted Peter there. Mark then left Rome, probably after Peter was martyred, but returned when Paul asked for him during his second imprisonment there. With the temporary exception of Paul during their brief conflict, it appears Mark's contemporaries regarded him as a faithful and effective servant and missionary.

In the New Testament, we read about both Mark (Acts 12:12) and John Mark (Acts 13:5). Both are thought to be the same man, author of the Gospel of Mark. The first usage is his

Gentile (Latin) name, while the latter combines his Jewish and Gentile names. Mark would have been called Yochanan (pronounced *yo-ka-non*) while in Jerusalem and Marcus when in Rome.

THE GOSPEL OF PETER?

One of the most striking characteristics of Mark's Gospel is its vividness. Like any great storyteller, Mark fills his account with memorable details that an eyewitness could most easily provide: Jesus spent His time in the desert "with the wild beasts" (Mark 1:13 NKJV); He went to pray "in the morning, having risen a long while before daylight" (1:35 NKJV); in the midst of a storm, Jesus lay in a boat "asleep on a pillow" (4:38 NKJV).

The forceful and descriptive style of Mark's writing also supports the idea of an eyewitness source. He employs the Greek historical present tense more than one hundred fifty times and the term *immediately,* or its variations, forty-two times in his Gospel.

Most scholars agree that Mark's eyewitness source must have been Peter. He knew Peter personally and would have heard him preach many times. Peter himself testified to the closeness of their relationship when he sent greetings to his readers from "Mark my son" (1 Peter 5:13 NKJV). Mark was described by some as Peter's "interpreter," probably meaning he explained Peter's teaching to a wider audience by writing it down. Many of this Gospel's details could have been provided only by a member of Jesus' inner circle, and Peter's words and deeds figure prominently in Mark's narrative. The outline of events in Mark's Gospel even follows the outline of one of Peter's recorded sermons (Acts 10:34–43).

Though most of the Gospel of Mark seems to be presented from Peter's perspective—it almost could have been titled "The Gospel According to Peter"—it appears the author inserted at least one personal detail. When Mark describes a young man fleeing naked from the scene of Jesus' arrest (Mark 14:51–52), many scholars believe he is referring to none other than himself.

THE ORDER OF THINGS

It's important to note that although the chronology of events in Mark closely follows the order listed in the other three Gospels, it doesn't always match precisely. In addition, some incidents within the book of Mark follow each other so neatly (as in chapter 12) that a reader might be tempted to question whether things really happened that way.

None of the Gospels, however, was intended to be a strict biography of the life of Jesus. Rather, each author drew from the known incidents of Jesus' life on earth to emphasize whatever point he was trying to make. The message was considered more important than the preservation of an exact chronology. Papias, the early church bishop, was quoted as saying that Mark wrote down the teachings of Peter, "not in any particular order but as he remembered them."

The book of Mark is one of the three "synoptic" Gospels, along with Matthew and Luke, so named because each narrative is similar in presentation and viewpoint. The book of John is different in that the author was more selective in what he recorded and focused more on explaining rather than relating events.

Despite their slight variations in emphasis, the Gospels as a group are in remarkable agreement about the events and details of the life of Jesus—as much, or more so, than a comparison of many eyewitness accounts of events recorded today.

A DEBATE OVER DATES

Unlike the identity of the author of Mark, the question of when this Gospel was written has been a matter of historical debate. For most Bible scholars, the range in question is only a matter of some twelve years. The issue is whether Mark set down the words of Peter's preaching *before* the death of the apostle or after his passing. Peter is thought to have been martyred in Rome sometime during AD 64–68. The most common dates ascribed to the writing of Mark are either AD 57–59 or AD 67–69. Either way, the events described in Mark were recorded only three or four decades after the fact—from the perspective of history, practically an on-the-spot retelling. Yet another matter that once stirred debate is whether Mark was the *first* Gospel written. From the fourth until the nineteenth centuries, the text was largely ignored by scholars because it was commonly considered an abridgement to Matthew. But a close examination of both Matthew and Luke seems to show that the authors of these Gospels used Mark as a source for their work, not the other way around. Since the end of the nineteenth century, most scholars have agreed that Mark was the first Gospel recorded.

Less controversial is the question of *where* Mark originated. Early church fathers almost universally testified that Mark was written in Rome, and few have found reason to dispute their testimony since. In addition, the content of Mark's narrative points to an audience of Roman Christians. For example, Jewish customs are explained; several Latin terms, not their Greek equivalents, are used; the Roman method of reckoning time is included; and the tone and message seem intended for an audience encountering persecution and expecting more— exactly the circumstances of Rome's Christians at the time.

JESUS CHRIST: HOLY YET HUMAN

In the very first sentence of his Gospel, Mark identifies Jesus as the "Son of God" and spends the rest of his narrative demonstrating why we, his readers, should come to the same conclusion. He introduces us to John the Baptist, who announces, "There comes One after me who is mightier than I" (Mark 1:7 NKJV). He shows us Jesus' command over demons and disease (1:21–45). He includes miracles demonstrating the Messiah's sovereign power (4:35–5:43). He records Peter's confession that Jesus is the Christ (8:29). And, of course, he takes us through Jesus' betrayal, trials, crucifixion, burial, and resurrection (14:43–16). Throughout his text, Mark is careful to emphasize Jesus' authority and divinity as God's representative on earth.

PERSECUTION IN ROME

If you were a Christian, Rome was not a good place to be at the time Mark was writing his Gospel. Nero, who ruled over the Roman Empire from AD 54 to 68, was a cruel and self-indulgent emperor. He even ordered the murder of his own mother when he felt she interfered too much in political affairs. After a major fire in Rome in AD 64, he offended the citizenry by erecting a hedonistic "Golden House" in the center of the city. Many believed he set the fire himself in order to clear the ground for his new project.

When the rumors of arson persisted, Nero tried to blame the fire on Christians and inflicted terrible punishments on them. Some were crucified, torn apart by dogs, or set on fire to be used as torches at night. It was probably Nero who ordered the executions of Peter and Paul. Though the general population looked down on Christians, the emperor's persecution of them was so brutal that he alienated the citizens of Rome.

By AD 68, Nero had lost the confidence of many of his military commanders throughout the empire. The Roman Senate declared Nero an outlaw. He took his own life that same year to escape a painful and degrading death.

Mark's many references to suffering and discipleship may very well have been specific instruction and preparation for a Roman Christian audience during these hard times.

At the same time, however, Mark contrasts this emphasis with a focus on Jesus' humanity and humility as a servant. No other book of the Bible gives us as complete a picture of the emotional side of Christ. We see His compassion, displeasure, and anger. We also learn of His distress in the moments before His arrest in the Garden of Gethsemane: "My soul is exceedingly sorrowful, even to death" (Mark 14:34 NKJV).

Perhaps even more important, we learn just as the disciples did two thousand years ago what it means to follow Jesus: "Whoever desires to become great among you shall be your servant. And whoever of you desires to be first shall be slave of all" (Mark 10:43–44 NKJV). Jesus turns the world's value system upside down. Mark reveals that the life of discipleship is to be characterized by humble and loving service.

How This Study Guide Is Organized

There are many methods to choose from when delving deeper into the Bible, including a topical study of major subjects or a verse-by-verse examination. As with other study guides in the Nelson Impact Bible Study Series, however, we have chosen the sequential approach. We will examine the text in front-to-back order with our chapters divided by the location of Jesus and His disciples. We begin in the wilderness with Jesus preparing for His public ministry. We follow Him through both early and later periods of ministry in Galilee, then observe His teaching and miracles in Galilee and beyond. We travel with Jesus on His journey to Jerusalem and then witness His ministry there. Finally, in our last three chapters, we study the events surrounding His historic crucifixion, death, and resurrection.

As you read through the vivid account of these events while using this study guide, imagine what it would have been like to be on the scene with the disciples, seeing and hearing with your own eyes and ears the incredible words and deeds of this man—this Messiah—named Jesus. Even if you have been a Christian for many years, your study of the Gospel of Mark may help you discover Jesus anew and draw you closer than ever before to the King of kings and Lord of lords.

The 35 Miracles of Jesus Christ, as Reported in the Four Gospels

		Matt.	Mark	Luke	John
1	Turning water into wine, at Cana				2:1–11
2	Healing an official's son, at Capernaum				4:46–54
3	Delivering a demoniac in the synagogue, at Capernaum		1:21–28	4:33–37	
4	Healing Peter's wife's mother, at Capernaum	8:14–15	1:29–31	4:38–39	
5	First miraculous catch of fish, at the Sea of Galilee			5:1–11	
6	Cleansing a leper, in Galilee	8:2–4	1:40–45	5:12–15	
7	Healing a paralytic, at Capernaum	9:1–8	2:1–12	5:17–26	
8	Healing an infirm man at the Pool of Bethesda, in Jerusalem				5:1-15
9	Healing a man's withered hand, in Galilee	12:9–13	3:1–5	6:6–11	
10	Healing a centurion's servant, at Capernaum	8:5–13		7:1–10	
11	Raising a widow's son, at Nain			7:11–17	
12	Casting out a blind and dumb spirit, in Galilee	12:22–32		11:14–23	
13	Stilling a storm, on the Sea of Galilee	8:18–27	4:35–41	8:22–25	
14	Delivering a demoniac of Gadara, at Gadara	8:28–34	5:1–20	8:26–39	
15	Healing a woman with a hemorrhage, at Capernaum	9:20–22	5:25–34	8:43–48	
16	Raising Jairus's daughter, at Capernaum	9:18–26	5:22–43	8:41–56	
17	Healing two blind men, at Capernaum	9:27–31			
18	Casting out a dumb spirit, at Capernaum	9:32–34			
19	Feeding the 5,000, near Bethsaida	14:13–21	6:32–44	9:10–17	6:1–14
20	Walking on the water, on the Sea of Galilee	14:22–33	6:45–52		6:15–21
21	Casting a demon from a Syrophoenician's daughter, at Phoenicia	15:21–28	7:24–30		
22	Healing a deaf person with a speech impediment, at Decapolis		7:31–37		
23	Feeding the 4,000, at Decapolis	15:32–38	8:1–9		
24	Healing a blind man of Bethsaida, at Bethsaida		8:22–26		
25	Casting out a demon from a lunatic boy, on Mount Hermon	17:14–21	9:14–29	9:37–42	
26	Finding money in a fish's mouth, at Capernaum	17:24–27			
27	Healing a man born blind, in Jerusalem				9:1–7
28	Healing a woman infirm for 18 years, probably at Perea			13:10–17	
29	Healing a man with dropsy, at Perea			14:1–6	
30	Raising Lazarus, at Bethany				11:1–44
31	Cleansing 10 lepers, in Samaria			17:11–19	
32	Healing blind Bartimaeus, at Jericho	20:29–34	10:46–52	18:35–43	
33	Cursing a fig tree, in Jerusalem	21:18–19	11:12–14		
34	Healing Malchus's ear, in the Garden of Gethsemane in Jerusalem			22:49–51	
35	Second miraculous catch of fish, on the Sea of Galilee				21:1–13
	Totals	**20**	**18**	**20**	**8**

1

PREPARING FOR PUBLIC MINISTRY

MARK 1:1–13

Before We Begin ...

What do you believe was God's mission for John the Baptist? How do you think John reacted when he realized who Jesus was?

In the very first sentence of his Gospel, Mark makes a point of introducing his main character—Jesus—with a specific title: "Jesus Christ, the Son of God." Every word in this introduction bears significant meaning.

Jesus, a divinely given personal name, is the Greek equivalent of *Yhosua* (Joshua) in Hebrew and means "Yahweh is salvation."

Christ is the Greek equivalent of the Hebrew title *mashiyach* (messiah), meaning "anointed one." It refers to the ruler and deliverer anticipated by the Jewish people who would fulfill Old Testament prophecies. The title *Christ* eventually became part of Jesus' personal name.

Son points to Jesus' unique relationship to God, as well as to His humanity. He depends on and obeys God the Father just as a human son does his father.

God emphasizes Jesus' deity. Though He has adopted human form according to His Father's plan, He remains perfect, holy, and fully divine.

Think about what Mark may have been trying to communicate by starting out his narrative this way, then answer the following questions.

What effect might the name Jesus have had on people who met Him and understood its meaning? What other meanings of names might God have considered for His only Son?

What does a title say about a person? How can a title be misleading?

Does the idea of Jesus as "Son of God" make it easier or harder for you to identify with Him? Why?

How can someone be both human and divine? List any struggles you might have with this concept.

GETTING READY (MARK 1:1–8)

The first section of the Gospel of Mark is all about "getting ready." John the Baptist prepares the people for the arrival of a new king—the King of *all* kings—with proclamations to great crowds of people. Jesus prepares for His historic ministry through His baptism and through a period of testing in the desert. The actions of both are vital to the success of everything that follows.

Before describing these events, however, Mark readies his own readers for what is to come. He reminds us of the Old Testament prophecies about a messenger who will "prepare the way of the LORD" (Mark 1:3 NKJV) as recorded by the prophet Isaiah. Other than quotations by Jesus, it is the only place in his Gospel where Mark refers to the Old Testament.

Fill in the blanks in the passage below, then answer the questions that follow.

"Behold, I send My _____ before Your face,

Who will _____ Your way before You."

"The voice of one crying in the _____:

'Prepare the way of the LORD;

Make His _____ straight.'"

(Mark 1:2–3 NKJV)

In ancient times, often a messenger was sent ahead to announce the coming of a king so townspeople could repair rough roads. How is John the Baptist like one of these messengers?

In what ways might people have responded differently to Jesus if John the Baptist had not "prepared the way"?

Do you see any similarities between the Israelites' wanderings in the wilderness and God's chosen messenger, John the Baptist? What are they?

Why does Mark seem to emphasize the "journey" aspect of Jesus' ministry by repeatedly employing terms such as "way" and "paths"?

JOHN AND JESUS IN THE JORDAN RIVER (MARK 1:9–11)

In Mark 1:4–5, we learn that John was baptizing huge crowds—imagine long lines of people waiting for their turn in the Jordan River—and preaching "repentance for the remission of sins" (v. 4 NKJV). But Mark quickly points out the contrast we will see between these people, as well as John himself, and the One who was coming. John told the people, "There comes One after me who is mightier than I, whose sandal strap I am not worthy to stoop down and loose. I indeed baptized you with water, but He will baptize you with the Holy Spirit" (Mark 1:7–8 NKJV).

The contrast becomes more apparent when we read about Jesus' arrival and baptism. The text doesn't mention that Jesus sought forgiveness of sins, because he didn't need forgiveness. Then, after He emerged from the river, the heavens themselves responded: "He saw the heavens parting and the Spirit descending upon Him like a dove. Then a voice came from heaven, 'You are My beloved Son, in whom I am well pleased'" (Mark 1:10–11 NKJV).

Even a Hebrew slave was not required to perform a task as menial as loosening the straps of his master's sandals. Why did John the Baptist (and Mark) make such a point of this humbling illustration?

Why do you think it was important for John to introduce a "baptism of repentance" just before the ministry of Jesus?

Why would Jesus, who was already one with God, submit Himself to John's baptism?

How was Jesus clearly set apart from everyone else who was baptized that day?

esu A NEW KIND OF BAPTISM

John the Baptist preached of the need for a "baptism of repentance" (Mark 1:4 NKJV), specifically "for the remission [or forgiveness] of sins" (v. 4 NKJV). *Repentance (metanoia* in Greek) means "a turn about, a deliberate change of mind resulting in a change of direction and thought and behavior," while *forgiveness (aphesin* in Greek) means "the removal or cancellation of an obligation or barrier of guilt." The rite of baptism itself did not bring about forgiveness but was a public sign that one had repented and been forgiven of sins by God.

The concept of baptism was nothing new to the people of Judea, but John's assertion that baptism was designed for the Jews and required repentance certainly was! Yet every Jew familiar with the history of Israel knew its people had fallen short of God's commands. The size of the crowds that followed John indicated that the people were ready to confess their disobedience and turn anew to God.

THE DEVIL IN THE DESERT (MARK 1:12–13)

The next two verses tell of Jesus' forty-day time of testing and temptation in the wilderness. The number forty recalls the experiences of Moses (Exod. 24:18) and Elijah (1 Kings 19:8), as well as Israel's forty-year trial in the desert. Here, in a place populated by "wild beasts" and characterized by desolation, loneliness, and danger, Jesus encounters the prince of evil personally. Yet Jesus is not alone; He is attended by angels, reminding us that God is always with us no matter how desperate our circumstances.

Why would God allow Satan to tempt Jesus just before the beginning of His ministry?

TESTING, TESTING

When Mark wrote about Jesus' temptation in the wilderness, he used a form of the Greek word *peirazo*, which means "to put to the test" or "to make trial of." He was referring to an ordeal designed for discovering what kind of person someone is. The test might come from God, as when He commanded Abraham to sacrifice his son as a test of his faith (Gen. 22:2), or from Satan as an enticement to sin.

In the case of Jesus' trial in the wilderness, both kinds of tests were involved. Through the Holy Spirit's leading, God put Jesus to the test to prepare Him for the days ahead and to show that He was ready for His earthly ministry. Satan attempted to distract Jesus from that ministry and thwart God's holy plan. This effort failed, of course.

It's important to realize, however, that Jesus *was* tempted by Satan, just as we all are—particularly when we are doing the most good or are most vulnerable. The sin, thankfully, is not in *encountering* temptation but in *yielding* to it. And as we learn from the apostle Paul (1 Cor. 10:13), God always offers an escape from the devil's snare.

Why are Mark's final words in this passage—"and the angels ministered to Him"—so important?

PULLING IT ALL TOGETHER . . .

• The first section of Mark is about *preparation.* As was prophesied by Isaiah and others in the Old Testament, God sent a messenger—John the Baptist—to prepare the way for the Lord. John introduced a new form of baptism that called for repentance and forgiveness of sins. The people of Judea responded, coming out in droves to the wilderness to be baptized in the Jordan River. There, John announced to the people that someone even mightier than he was coming who would baptize not with water but with the Holy Spirit. Though they didn't realize it, John was preparing the people for a Savior.

• A man named Jesus then came to John and was baptized. The heavens opened up and God Himself spoke, publicly identifying Jesus as His Son and describing His love for and delight in Him.

• Jesus then went deeper into the wilderness, where He was tempted by Satan and attended by angels for forty days. This was a time of testing and preparation for Jesus—His final moments before beginning a ministry that would change the course of history.

2

EARLY GALILEAN MINISTRY

MARK 1:14–3:6

Before We Begin . . .

If Jesus had begun His ministry today instead of two thousand years ago, would you have embraced Him as the disciples did or opposed Him as the Pharisees did? Why?

In Mark's record of the beginning of Jesus' public ministry, we are introduced to the major elements that appear in most of the rest of his Gospel: Jesus teaching and working with His disciples; Jesus preaching to the people; Jesus performing miracles such as healing and driving out demons; and Jesus coming into conflict with authorities.

Jesus launched His ministry with an important public statement. Upon arriving in Galilee, one of the largest Roman districts of Palestine, Jesus began preaching the gospel and announced, "The time is fulfilled, and the kingdom of God is at hand. Repent, and believe in the gospel" (Mark 1:15 NKJV).

KEY PLACES IN JESUS' GALILEAN MINISTRY

ITUREA

Tyre

Caesarea Philippi

PHOENICIA

GALILEE

Chorazin
Gennesaret Bethsaida?
Capernaum
Cana Magdala Sea of Galilee
Tiberias

Nazareth Mt. Tabor

Nain Gadara?

DECAPOLIS

Jordan River

SAMARIA

0   20 Mi.
0   20 Km.

? Exact location questionable

© 2006 Thomas Nelson, Inc.

This statement includes two declarations and two commands. The first declaration, "The time is fulfilled," indicates that the preparation and expectation of the Old Testament era were over. A new era was dawning.

What would this statement have meant to Jesus' listeners?

The second declaration, "The kingdom of God is at hand," alluded to the coming of a royal, holy, and sovereign ruler. The Jews were expecting a future messianic kingdom to be established on earth, so they would have understood this reference. But it's doubtful they realized that the messenger before them, Jesus, was the King they were waiting for!

Why would it have been difficult for the Jewish people to accept Jesus as a king?

The first command issued by Jesus is "Repent," which in this usage means to turn away from an existing object of trust, such as oneself.

Why would Jesus have opened his ministry with a command as challenging as "Repent"?

The second command is "believe in the gospel." "Believe" meant to commit oneself completely to an object of faith, while "gospel" referred to the good news of Jesus Christ as Savior and Messiah.

Why didn't Jesus immediately explain to His listeners that He was the good news they were seeking?

FISHERMEN-TURNED-DISCIPLES (MARK 1:16–20)

We meet Peter, the future "rock" of the church then known as Simon, for the first time in Mark's Gospel when Jesus sees him fishing with his brother Andrew beside the Sea of Galilee. Jesus doesn't hesitate to recruit them, saying, "Follow Me, and I will make you become fishers of men" (Mark 1:17 NKJV).

Would you be willing to walk away from your livelihood on a moment's notice? What would have convinced Peter and Andrew to follow Jesus so quickly?

It's interesting that the phrase "Follow Me" could be translated here as "Go behind Me as a disciple." Jesus did not act like a traditional rabbi, waiting for students to seek him out, but instead pursued and singled out the men who would become His closest followers.

Why did Jesus choose common fishermen as His first disciples? Why does Mark take the time to tell us about their profession?

Jesus promised to make his disciples "fishers of men." The metaphor echoes Isaiah's words describing the wicked as being like the "troubled sea," with "no peace" (Isa. 57:20–21).

Why is Jesus' sea metaphor such an apt one for the future work of His disciples?

Perhaps only a few minutes after encountering Simon and Andrew, Jesus spies James and his brother John in a fishing boat. He calls them to discipleship as well: both "left their father Zebedee in the boat with the hired servants, and went after Him" (Mark 1:20 NKJV).

Mark immediately follows Jesus' commands to repent and believe with the accounts of Jesus gathering His first disciples, including the details about James and John leaving their father and his hired hands behind. What is Mark saying here about the commitment required for discipleship?

ONE AMAZING DAY (MARK 1:21–34)

In the following fourteen verses, the four fishermen-turned-disciples quickly discovered new evidence that this Jesus was unlike anyone they had encountered before. Jesus entered the synagogue and taught as one with authority. He sent unclean spirits out of a man (the first of the eighteen miracles recorded in Mark). He removed the fever of Simon's mother-in-law. In the evening, the "whole city" gathered at His door, bringing their sick and demon-possessed, and He healed them.

Read Mark 1:21–34 and pay special attention to the responses Jesus' actions elicited from His new disciples and from others.

What kind of thoughts must have been running through the minds of Simon, Andrew, James, and John at the end of this amazing day?

How was it more powerful for Jesus to teach in the synagogue with authority, drive out demons, and heal the sick than to simply announce to the crowds that He was the Messiah?

How did these early authoritative deeds and miracles prepare the people of Galilee (as well as Mark's readers) to hear and receive Jesus' message?

Even in an age before radio, television, and the Internet, word of Jesus' incredible deeds spread quickly. How did Jesus' fame differ from that of celebrities today?

Mark provides very specific details about the time when "the whole city" came to Jesus with their sick and demon-possessed, noting that it was "at evening, when the sun had set" (Mark 1:32 NKJV). This reference shows that the people of Capernaum waited until the Sabbath day was over, after sunset, before transporting anyone. The law and rabbinic regulations prohibited any work from being performed on the Sabbath.

What is your response to the powerful picture of perhaps hundreds of desperate people waiting impatiently for the sun to go down so they could have a chance at healing?

Origin of the Synagogue

The synagogue (from the Greek *sunagoge,* meaning "a leading or bringing together") originated when Jewish captives in Babylon, lacking a temple but longing for communion with God, met in small groups to worship and read the Torah. The practice grew until synagogues became centers of community life. Some served as grammar schools and courts of justice; all provided an important theological and social function.

The synagogue had a significant impact on early Christian worship. In the Jewish service, the speaker for the day led attendees in prayer as they stood facing Jerusalem with hands extended. The speaker read the Law while an interpreter translated his words into Aramaic. A passage from the Prophets was read and translated. Then the speaker sat down and delivered a sermon. After the sermon, a priest pronounced a benediction; the people responded with an "Amen."

Since the first Christians were Jews, they often followed this pattern for their own worship gatherings.

Prayer and Preaching (Mark 1:35–45)

Fill in the blanks in the passage below.

Now in the morning, having risen a long while before daylight, He went out and _____ to a solitary place; and there He _____. And Simon and those who were with Him _____ for Him. When they found Him, they said to Him, "Everyone is _____ for You." But He said to them, "Let us go into the next towns, that I may _____ there also, because for this _____ I have come forth." And He was _____ in their synagogues throughout all Galilee, and casting out demons. (Mark 1:35–39 NKJV)

What is Mark telling us about the importance of prayer in this passage?

Why did Jesus decide to move on instead of staying in Capernaum?

Read Mark 1:40–45, then answer the following questions.

How strong was the leper's faith?

Why was Jesus' touch a significant demonstration of compassion (see Lev. 13:45–46)?

SECRET IDENTITY?

Many explanations have been offered for Jesus' admonition to the leper to "say nothing to anyone" (Mark 1:44 NKJV), though none can be proven conclusively. For example:

1. Jesus was careful to keep His identity secret to avoid misconceptions about what the work of the Messiah would be. This view is called the "messianic secret."
2. Jesus did not want to be seen only as a miracle worker.
3. Jesus didn't want His teaching ministry hindered by too much publicity.
4. Jesus didn't want to set events in motion that would bring about His death prematurely, before He had finished His ministry.
5. A report of Jesus' healing of the leper might have prejudiced the priest who needed to pronounce him clean.

Whatever the reason, Jesus' words were in vain, because the leper spread the news freely (a common occurrence in the book of Mark). One result was that Jesus could no longer enter cities openly. Instead, He stayed in "deserted places" and the multitudes came to Him.

CONFLICT WITH JEWISH RELIGIOUS LEADERS (MARK 2:1–3:5)

In Mark 2:1–3:5, we observe a striking contrast in the responses Jesus was provoking in Galilee. The previous passages are filled with examples of amazement and growing faith inspired by the words and deeds of Jesus. His popularity with the people was soaring; huge crowds followed Him everywhere.

But Jesus' actions had also attracted the attention of Jewish religious leaders, and their reaction took a very different course. The following section includes five examples of the increasing conflict between Jesus and the Jewish leadership.

1. FORGIVING SIN (MARK 2:1–12)

Jesus, preaching in a house in Capernaum, responded to the tenacity and faith of four men carrying a paralytic. He healed him by simply saying, "Son, your sins are forgiven you" (Mark 2:5 NKJV). The teachers of the Law were shocked, believing this to be blasphemy. Jesus showed them that He had the authority to forgive sin by instructing the paralytic to walk.

Mark makes a clear distinction between the faith of the paralytic and his four friends and the faith of the scribes. Why did these teachers of the Law struggle so hard against what they were seeing and hearing?

In the Old Testament, disease was considered a consequence of a man's sinful condition. Why, instead of only healing the paralytic, did Jesus also make a point of forgiving his sins?

23

Why did Jesus ask which is easier, forgiving sin or healing a paralytic?

2. EATING WITH SINNERS (MARK 2:13–17)

Jesus recruited Levi the tax collector, also known as Matthew, to join His band of disciples. As they dined together with many other tax collectors and sinners, scribes and Pharisees questioned why Jesus associated with these outcasts. Jesus replied, "I did not come to call the righteous, but sinners, to repentance" (Mark 2:17 NKJV).

Jesus had already included common fishermen in His group of followers. Now He invited one of the tax collectors—servants of the government, often corrupt, and despised by the Jews—to join Him. What kind of statement was Jesus making here?

The Pharisees did not confront Jesus with their complaints about His eating with sinners, but mentioned them to the disciples instead. Why do you think they did this?

Based on this passage, how do you think the Pharisees viewed themselves?

THE PHARISEES

Both scribes and priests could be found among the religious leaders known as Pharisees. They were Jews who joined forces with the Maccabees during the struggle for freedom from Syrian oppression (166–144 BC). The first known appearance of this group under the name "Pharisee" was during the reign of John Hyrcanus (135–105 BC).

At the time of Mark's Gospel, the Pharisees were the most influential religious party in Palestine. Those who came into conflict with Jesus were legalistic, hypocritical, and envious. According to their interpretation of Judaic tradition, God's grace extended only to those who kept His law. They criticized Jesus for failing to distinguish between the "righteous" (in their view, themselves) and the "sinners."

It's likely that many Pharisees were more godly than those who confronted and opposed Jesus. Most scholars, in fact, believe that Jesus was a Pharisee Himself, in part because many of His teachings paralleled the words of well-known Pharisee scholars of history.

3. FAILING TO FAST (MARK 2:18–22)

Disciples of John the Baptist and the Pharisees were fasting and asked Jesus why His followers didn't fast as well. Jesus answered, "As long as they have the bridegroom with them they cannot fast" (Mark 2:19 NKJV). He then explained further by telling the parable of old and new wineskins.

For the disciples, how was being with Jesus like being at a wedding?

What was Jesus hinting at when He said, "The days will come when the bridegroom will be taken away from them" (Mark 2:20 NKJV)?

What is the meaning of the wineskins parable?

4. Plucking Grain on the Sabbath (Mark 2:23–28)

Jesus and His disciples were walking through grain fields on the Sabbath when the disciples began to pick heads of grain. The Pharisees asked Jesus why they were breaking Sabbath law. Jesus pointed to the precedent set by David in the Old Testament (1 Sam. 21:1–6) and said, "The Sabbath was made for man, and not man for the Sabbath. Therefore the Son of Man is also Lord of the Sabbath" (Mark 2:27–28 NKJV).

How were David's actions like those of the disciples?

Was Jesus saying that it's more important to obey the Spirit than the letter of the law?

What did He mean when He said, "The Sabbath was made for man"?

5. HEALING ON THE SABBATH (MARK 3:1–5)

Jesus entered a synagogue on the Sabbath. A man with a withered hand was there; so were the Pharisees, watching closely to see what Jesus would do. Jesus asked the Pharisees, "Is it lawful on the Sabbath to do good or to do evil, to save life or to kill?" (Mark 3:4 NKJV). Their silence provoked Jesus' anger before He healed the man.

At this point, were the Pharisees watching Jesus in order to learn from Him or to condemn Him?

Was Jesus asking the Pharisees a legal question or a moral one? Which is more important in God's eyes?

How was Jesus' anger appropriate in light of the circumstances?

JESUS REJECTED BY THE PHARISEES (MARK 3:6)

Mark concludes his account of Jesus' five conflicts with Jewish religious leaders with this statement: "Then the Pharisees went out and immediately plotted with the Herodians against Him, how they might destroy Him" (Mark 3:6 NKJV). It is a turning point in his Gospel, as it is the first explicit reference to Jesus' death.

Why were the Pharisees so threatened by Jesus?

27

The Herodians were Jewish supporters of Herod Antipas and Roman rule. Why would they have joined forces with the Pharisees to oppose Jesus?

PULLING IT ALL TOGETHER . . .

• Jesus began His public ministry with a statement—part declaration and part command—that summarized His mission on earth. He began formulating His inner circle, common fishermen and one tax collector, who would become disciples and, later, apostles.

• Through His authoritative preaching and miracles of healing and exorcism, Jesus displayed the evidence that He was God's agent.

• Jesus' fame and influence grew quickly; great crowds of people followed Him everywhere. When Jesus declared His authority over traditional Judaic laws, however, He found enemies in the Pharisees, who began plotting with the Herodians to kill Him.

What motivated these people to walk many miles to see Jesus? Was it faith? Hope for healing? Mere curiosity?

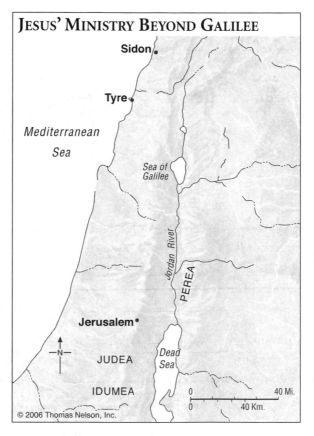

In Mark 3:11–12, we see that "unclean spirits" recognized Jesus for who He was, yet He ordered them to keep this knowledge to themselves.

How was it that the demons identified the Son of God before His own followers did? What does this say about humanity in general?

LATER GALILEAN MINISTRY

MARK 3:7–6:6

Before We Begin . . .

The term miracle *is often ascribed today to relatively common events such as an impressive comeback at a football game or a salary increase at work. In light of the miracles of Jesus, what does this word mean to you?*

Over parts of the next four chapters in the book of Mark, we observe the "commissioning" of the disciples and an expansion of Jesus' ministry. We also discover more about the character of God's kingdom and the power and authority of Jesus through four parables and four miracles.

In Mark 3:7–8, we learn that great crowds followed Jesus wherever He went. They came not only from the vicinity of Capernaum, but also from considerable distances—to the south, from Jerusalem and all of Judea, and even the region of Idumea more than one hundred miles away; to the east, from Perea; and to the north, from the cities of Tyre and Sidon on the Mediterranean coast (see the map on the following page to get a better idea of how far people traveled to see Jesus). Jesus' popularity became so great that He arranged for a small boat to be ready in case the crowds moved in to crush Him.

Have you ever been so tightly packed in a crowd that you feared for your life?

THE TWELVE APOSTLES (MARK 3:13–19)

Read Mark 3:13–19, then answer the following questions.

What are the four purposes listed by Mark for appointing the apostles?

1.

2.

3.

4.

Why did Jesus change Simon's name to Peter?

Why did Jesus choose to give His closest instruction to only twelve men? Why not fifty or one hundred?

JESUS AND BEELZEBUB (MARK 3:20–27)

When Jesus' "own people"—perhaps His family from Nazareth—heard that He didn't even have time to eat, they came to care for Him. Meanwhile, scribes from Jerusalem accused Jesus of an alliance with Beelzebub, or Satan.

Fill in the blanks in the passage below, then answer the questions that follow.

And the scribes who came down from Jerusalem said, "He has _____," and, "By the ruler of the _____ He casts out _____." So He called them to Himself and said to them in parables: "How can _____ cast out Satan? If a kingdom is divided against itself, that kingdom cannot _____. And if a house is divided against itself, that house cannot _____. And if Satan has risen up against himself, and is divided, he cannot stand, but has an _____. No one can enter a strong man's house and plunder his goods, unless he first _____ the strong man. And then he will plunder his house." (Mark 3:22–27 NKJV)

How did Jesus refute the scribes' charges that He was driving out demons with demons?

What did Jesus say would happen to Satan if he opposed himself?

Who is the strong man in the analogy in Mark 3:27? Who has come to bind him?

THE UNPARDONABLE SIN (MARK 3:28–30)

The opening phrase of Mark 3:28—"Assuredly, I say to you"—
is one of thirteen solemn introductions uttered by Jesus in this
Gospel. It means that a statement of great truth and import is
coming—and, indeed, Jesus followed these words with a harsh
condemnation of the scribes and a warning to all who would
equate the power of God with Satan: "Assuredly, I say to you,
all sins will be forgiven the sons of men, and whatever blas-
phemies they may utter; but he who blasphemes against the
Holy Spirit never has forgiveness, but is subject to eternal condemnation"—because they said, "He has an unclean spirit"
(Mark 3:28–30 NKJV).

*Why would God regard blasphemy against the Holy Spirit as the
one unpardonable sin?*

*Was Jesus condemning a single blasphemy or an attitude of defi-
ance toward God?*

JESUS' TRUE FAMILY (MARK 3:31–35)

At the end of chapter 3, Mark returns to the narrative of 3:21,
describing the arrival of Jesus' mother and brothers. They
asked Him to come outside to speak, but He used the opportunity to make a point about membership in the family of
God.

Read Mark 3:31–35, then answer the following questions.

Was Jesus rejecting His earthly mother and brothers?

What qualifies someone for membership in Jesus' family?

Which family is clearly more important in the eyes of Jesus (see Mark 10:29–30)?

What sacrifices must sometimes be made within family relationships to stay obedient to God?

THE CHARACTER OF THE KINGDOM (MARK 4:1–32)

In chapter 4, Mark introduces four parables designed to reveal the character of God's kingdom. They were delivered amid Jesus' growing popularity among the people, as well as increasing opposition by the Pharisees and those who felt threatened politically by Jesus' rising influence.

esu THE STORY OF PARABLES

The word *parable* is a translation of the Greek *parabole,* meaning "comparison." Parables are usually stories from ordinary life used to illustrate spiritual or moral truth, sometimes in the form of brief similes, comparisons, analogies, or proverbial sayings. A parable usually explains a single important truth and invites its hearers to evaluate its truth for themselves. Parables were one of Jesus' favorite teaching techniques.

1. The Parable of the Sower (Mark 4:1–20)

Once again, Jesus was teaching a large crowd of people at the Sea of Galilee, this time sitting in a boat. Among the lessons he related is the parable of the sower.

Fill in the blanks in the passage below.

> "Listen! Behold, a _____ went out to sow. And it happened, as he sowed, that some seed _____ by the wayside; and the birds of the air came and _____ it. Some fell on stony ground, where it did not have much earth; and immediately it _____ up because it had no depth of earth. But when the sun was up it was _____, and because it had no root it _____ away. And some seed fell among thorns; and the thorns grew up and _____ it, and it yielded no crop. But other seed fell on _____ ground and yielded a crop that _____ up, _____ and _____: some thirtyfold, some sixty, and some a _____." And He said to them, "He who has _____ to hear, let him _____!" (Mark 4:3–9 NKJV)

What does this parable mean to you?

After the crowd left, the apostles and others asked Jesus about the meaning of the parable of the sower. He explained that those who have been chosen and those who are willing to believe can discover the mystery of the kingdom of God: that in Jesus, God's rule has come to earth in a new spiritual form. Those who have repeatedly hardened their hearts, however, will never understand the full meaning of the parables.

Jesus then compared such people to the Israelites in Isaiah's day. Isaiah said that their spiritual blindness and deafness was God's judgment: "Seeing they may see and not perceive, and hearing they may hear and not understand; lest they should turn, and their sins be forgiven them" (Mark 4:12 NKJV).

Why did Jesus conceal the true meaning of His parables from those who did not believe?

What is the connection between the words of Jesus in verse 9 and the words of Isaiah in verse 12?

Read Jesus' explanation of the parable of the sower in Mark 4:13–20, then answer the questions below.

Who is the sower in this parable?

What are the four ways that people respond to the message of Jesus in this parable?

1.

2.

3.

4.

Which type of seed are the Pharisees?

Which type of seed are the disciples?

Which kind of seed do you most identify with?

2. THE PARABLE OF THE LAMP (MARK 4:21–25)

Fill in the blanks, then answer the questions that follow.

> *Also He said to them, "Is a _____ brought to be put under a basket or under a bed? Is it not to be set on a _____? For there is nothing hidden which will not be _____, nor has anything been kept secret but that it should come to _____. If anyone has ears to hear, let him _____." Then He said to them, "Take _____ what you hear. With the same measure you use, it will be _____ to you; and to you who hear, more will be _____. For whoever has, to him _____ will be given; but whoever does not have, even what he has will be _____ away from him." (Mark 4:21–25 NKJV)*

In the first part of this passage, what kind of light was Jesus really talking about?

How is the Word of God sometimes hidden like a lampstand under a basket?

What reward awaits those who accept Jesus as the "light"?

What will happen to those who reject the light of Jesus?

3. THE PARABLE OF THE GROWING SEED (MARK 4:26–29)

Fill in the blanks, then answer the questions that follow.

> *And He said, "The kingdom of God is as if a man should _____ seed on the ground, and should _____ by night and rise by day, and the seed should _____ and grow, he himself does not know how. For the earth yields _____ by itself: first the _____, then the _____, after that the full _____ in the head. But when the grain ripens, immediately he puts in the _____, because the _____ has come." (Mark 4:26–29 NKJV)*

How is this parable like the parable of the sower?

Of the following three interpretations offered by scholars for this parable, which makes the most sense to you? Why?

1. A broad portrait of evangelism.

2. An example of spiritual growth in an individual believer.

3. A picture of the coming of God's kingdom through the sovereign work of God.

4. THE PARABLE OF THE MUSTARD SEED (MARK 4:30–32)

Fill in the blanks, then answer the questions that follow.

> *Then He said, "To what shall we liken the _____ of God? Or with what _____ shall we picture it? It is like a _____ seed which, when it is sown on the ground, is _____ than all the seeds on earth; but when it is sown, it _____ up and becomes _____ than all herbs, and shoots out large branches, so that the birds of the air may _____ under its shade." (Mark 4:30–32 NKJV)*

How is Jesus like the mustard seed in this parable?

When will Jesus most be like the fully grown mustard plant?

Whom do the birds represent?

THE MIGHTY MUSTARD SEED

The mustard seed was an appropriate illustration for Jesus' parable because it was the smallest of the seeds sown in the fields of Palestine. Between 725 and 760 mustard seeds would be required to produce a weight of just one gram. Yet the mustard shrub, an annual plant covered with yellow flowers, grew from seed to a height of twelve to fifteen feet in a few weeks. Mustard seeds were used to flavor meat and vegetables and were a favorite food of birds.

JESUS' USE OF PARABLES (MARK 4:33–34)

Jesus summarized His practice of speaking in parables in Mark 4:33–34. We also find out that He continued to explain the full meaning of His words to the disciples when they were alone.

Why do you think it was so difficult for the disciples to discern the truth behind Jesus' parables?

JESUS' SOVEREIGN POWER (MARK 4:35–5:43)

Mark follows up the four parables of Jesus with a series of four miracles demonstrating the power and authority of God's kingdom. Each miracle shows the Messiah's sovereignty over a different hostile force. Mark seems to be saying that Jesus' *words* would be backed up by His *deeds*—further proof that He is indeed the Son of God.

1. CALMING A STORM (MARK 4:35–41)

Jesus directed the disciples to leave the crowds behind and undertake a crossing of the Sea of Galilee in their boat. A tremendous storm arose, threatening to swamp the boat, yet an exhausted Jesus remained asleep on a pillow in the stern. The panicked disciples woke Him and cried, "Teacher, do You not care that we are perishing?" (Mark 4:38 NKJV).

THE SEA OF GALILEE

The Sea of Galilee (also called Lake Tiberias) is actually a freshwater lake eight miles across, renowned at the time of Mark's Gospel for its good fishing. Fishermen threw their drag nets by hand from small boats and dragged the nets along the bottom of the lake. Weights pulled down the edges of the nets to entrap the fish.

The sudden, furious squall that came upon Jesus and the disciples was not uncommon. Situated in a basin surrounded by mountains that rise as high as four thousand feet above sea level, the Sea of Galilee is still susceptible today to rapidly forming, violent storms. Cool air from the Mediterranean is drawn down through the narrow mountain passes. When it clashes with hot, humid air lying over the lake, it can stir up large waves treacherous for any sailor.

How could Jesus have slept through such a precarious situation?

What did He say to the wind and waves?

What was the result?

After calming the storm, Jesus had a sharp rebuke for his followers: "Why are you so fearful? How is it that you have no faith?" (Mark 4:40 NKJV).

Despite all that they had seen and heard, why did the disciples react with fear in the face of the storm?

What was the disciples' response to seeing Jesus' authority over creation itself?

Why do so many knowledgeable Christians today react just as the disciples did when life's storms strike?

2. HEALING A DEMON-POSSESSED MAN (MARK 5:1–20)

On the other side of the Sea of Galilee, Jesus and the disciples were met by a demon-possessed man. Jesus ordered the unclean spirit to come out of the man, then asked for its name. The man answered, "My name is Legion; for we are many" (Mark 5:9 NKJV).

Why was it apparent that this man was demon-possessed?

What was the man's first response upon seeing Jesus?

Why do we know that the demons recognized Jesus as the Son of God?

Read Mark 5:6–20, then answer the questions below.

What three requests did the demons make of Jesus?

1.

2.

3.

Which request did Jesus grant? What happened to the demons as a result?

What was the response of the people who saw that the demon-possessed man had been healed?

Why did these people wish that a miracle worker from God would leave their region?

Scholars have speculated that because the healed man was in a Gentile region where there was little chance that messianic theories about Jesus would circulate, He had no reason to ask the man to keep silent.

Why did Jesus refuse this man's request to be with Him?

3. HEALING AN AFFLICTED WOMAN (MARK 5:21–34)

Jesus was again surrounded by a crowd when a synagogue ruler, Jairus, broke through and begged Jesus to heal his dying daughter. Before they could go to her, however, a woman who had been afflicted for years by a flow of blood touched Jesus' clothing. She said, "If only I may touch His clothes, I shall be made well" (Mark 5:28 NKJV). Immediately the woman was healed.

What kind of struggles and suffering had this woman endured because of her affliction (see Lev. 15:25–27)?

The woman believed that merely touching Jesus' clothing would be enough to heal her. What does this say about the depth of her faith?

When the woman touched Jesus' garment, He responded by saying, "Who touched My clothes?" (Mark 5:30 NKJV). The fearful woman stepped forward and confessed the whole story. Jesus said to her, "Daughter, your faith has made you well. Go in peace, and be healed of your affliction" (Mark 5:34 NKJV).

What does this woman's healing tell us about Jesus' power, compassion, and sensitivity to faith?

Mark does not record the woman's response to her healing. How would you imagine it?

POWER GOING OUT

In the story of the healing of the afflicted woman, we read that Jesus, "immediately knowing in Himself that power had gone out of Him, turned around in the crowd and said, "Who touched My clothes?" (Mark 5:30 NKJV). "Knowing in Himself" comes from the Greek *epiginosko,* meaning "know fully." Translated more literally, it means "power from Him (on account of who He is) had gone out."

Scholars have generally interpreted this phrase in two ways. Some subscribe to the view that God healed the woman without Jesus' initial awareness. Others believe that Jesus purposely extended His healing power to her in order to reward her faith. In this view, His power would not depart Him without His knowledge or approval. The question "Who touched My clothes?" arose because Jesus wanted to publicly commend her for her faith and assure her that she was permanently healed.

In either case, scholars agree that the garment itself had no magical properties; it was the woman's faith that led to her healing.

It's also interesting to note that Jesus used the affectionate title "Daughter" for the woman (Mark 5:34). It is the only recorded use of the title by Jesus in the Bible, and probably indicated her new relationship with Jesus and standing in the family of God.

4. RESTORING A GIRL TO LIFE (MARK 5:21–24, 35–43)

While Jesus was speaking to the woman who had been healed, a delegation from the home of Jairus arrived and informed the synagogue leader that his daughter was dead. Jesus urged Jairus to hold on to his faith. They found a crowd weeping and wailing at the house. Jesus said, "Why make this commotion and weep? The child is not dead, but sleeping" (Mark 5:39 NKJV).

How was the report of his daughter's death a test of faith for Jairus?

What can we infer about the importance of faith from this story?

Why did Jesus tell the people that the girl was "sleeping"?

Jesus instructed everyone to leave the girl's room except for her parents and Peter, James, and John. In Aramaic, He told the daughter, "Little girl, I say to you, arise" (Mark 5:41 NKJV). To everyone's amazement, the girl immediately got up and began to walk. Jesus commanded them to keep quiet about the incident and said that the girl should be fed.

What impact do you think this incident had on the parents and on the three disciples?

What does it say about Jesus' authority?

JESUS REJECTED AT NAZARETH (MARK 6:1–6)

Read Mark 6:1–6, then answer the following questions.

When Jesus returned to teach in His hometown of Nazareth, what was the reaction of the people?

Even after they heard the wisdom of Jesus' teaching, why was it so hard for them to accept that He had the authority of God?

What did Jesus say in response? What does this mean?

Why could Jesus "do no mighty work" in Nazareth? Was His power truly limited?

Mark 6:6 is one of only two places in the Bible showing that Jesus was amazed at something. What did He marvel at in Nazareth?

PULLING IT ALL TOGETHER . . .

- Jesus' popularity grew to the point where He could barely move about the countryside because of the crowds.

- From the people who followed Him, He appointed twelve apostles.

- Jesus rebuked those who accused Him of being in league with Beelzebub and distinguished between His earthly family and His true family—that is, God's family.

- Mark then gives the account of four parables of Jesus that reveal the nature of God's kingdom. He follows this with the stories of four miracles that show the link between Jesus and the power and authority of God.

- Finally, Jesus returned to His hometown, only to find rejection by His own people.

- Throughout this section, we see the contrast between those of great faith (Jairus, the afflicted woman) and those of little faith (the disciples at the time of the storm at sea, the people of Nazareth). As it was for them, the same evidence is before us today. The question that arises is, will we choose to believe?

MINISTRY IN GALILEE AND BEYOND

MARK 6:7–8:30

Before We Begin . . .

Traditions are established patterns of thoughts, actions, or behaviors that provide a sense of assurance and connection with those who have gone before us. Is it possible, though, to cling too tightly to tradition? How could this lead to trouble?

In this next section of his Gospel, Mark recounts the continuing development of Jesus' ministry both in Galilee and in new regions. Jesus granted new responsibility and authority to His twelve disciples and gradually revealed even more of His true nature and mission. The section ends with Peter's realization and statement that Jesus is the Christ, or Messiah.

In Mark 6:7, Jesus for the first time sent out the Twelve to extend His ministry. He gave them authority over demons so the people would understand that they were His representatives and also had the authority of God.

What specific instructions did Jesus give the Twelve (vv. 8–10)?

Why would Jesus have wanted them to travel so unprepared, carrying not even food or money?

By shaking the dust off their feet, the disciples were warning people who would not listen that their responsibility to them had been fulfilled. What kind of judgment did Jesus promise these people?

What did the disciples learn about Jesus' authority as they preached and healed?

JOHN THE BAPTIST BEHEADED (MARK 6:14–29)

Over the next sixteen verses, Mark foreshadows Jesus' death and draws a parallel between John the Baptist and the Messiah.

Fill in the blanks below, then answer the questions that follow.

> *Now King Herod heard of Him, for His _____ had become well _____. And he said, "John the Baptist is _____ from the dead, and therefore these _____ are at work in him." Others said, "It is _____." And others said, "It is the _____, or like one of the prophets." But when Herod heard, he said, "This is _____, whom I beheaded; he has been raised from the _____!" For _____ himself had sent and laid hold of John, and bound him in _____ for the sake of _____, his brother Philip's wife; for he had _____ her. Because John had said to Herod, "It is not _____ for you to have your brother's wife." (Mark 6:14–18 NKJV)*

What three theories are presented here to explain Jesus' powers?

1.

2.

3.

Why was Herod convinced that Jesus was John, raised from the dead?

Why was John the Baptist so closely linked to Jesus?

Read Mark 6:19–29, the account of the death of John the Baptist, then answer the questions below.

What was Herod's opinion of John? Why?

What did Herodias think of John? Why?

Like Pontius Pilate in days to come, Herod was a reluctant executioner. What other parallels do you see between the unjust deaths of John the Baptist and Jesus?

HEROD'S HOUSE OF IMMORALITY

Herod Antipas, tetrarch of Galilee and Perea, was married to a daughter of an Arabian king when he became captivated by the daughter of his half brother, who was married to another half brother, Philip. So Herod divorced his wife to marry Herodias. John the Baptist denounced Herod's marriage to his half-niece, which was doubly immoral since sleeping with a brother's wife was viewed as incestuous as well as adulterous.

Herodias was apparently an ambitious, bitter, and manipulative woman. She nursed a grudge against John the Baptist for his stand against her second marriage, used her influence to have John imprisoned, and then through her daughter, Salome, tricked Herod into executing him. Later, she also convinced Herod to ask Caligula, the Roman emperor, for the title of king (the use of the title in Mark 6:14 may have been sarcastic). The emperor was so enraged at this request that he banished Herod to Gaul in AD 39. Herodias accompanied him into exile.

JESUS FEEDS THE FIVE THOUSAND (MARK 6:30–44)

Jesus and His disciples desperately needed food and rest, but the crowds of people now following Jesus would not give them time alone. Seeing the crowd, however, Jesus responded with compassion. He provided them with both kinds of the bread that we all need—bread for our physical bodies and the Bread of Life, Jesus Himself.

Read Mark 6:30–44, then answer the following questions.

In His compassion, how did Jesus view the crowd awaiting Him?

The disciples, perhaps emulating Jesus, also felt compassion for the people. What did they suggest?

When Jesus told the disciples to feed the crowd, how did they react?

How does Mark indicate that everyone had enough to eat?

Two Hundred Denarii

The Roman *denarius* was the most common coin in use at the time of Mark's Gospel. Struck from silver, it bore an imprint of the head of the emperor. Its value was the equivalent of an average daily wage for a farm laborer.

When the disciples said to Jesus, "Shall we go and buy two hundred denarii worth of bread and give them something to eat?" (Mark 6:37 NKJV), it meant they had calculated it would take roughly seven months' wages to feed the crowd—obviously far more than what they had on hand. The disciples' question could be seen as a sarcastic one.

Scholars believe that when Judas betrayed the Son of God for thirty pieces of silver, the coins were most likely denarii and roughly equal to a month's wages.

JESUS WALKS ON WATER (MARK 6:45–52)

After feeding the crowds, Jesus was finally able to retreat for some time alone to pray. The disciples were on a boat in the Sea of Galilee, making little headway because of a strong wind. Jesus decided to meet them.

And when they saw Him walking on the sea, they supposed it was a ghost, and cried out; for they all saw Him and were troubled. But immediately He talked with them and said to them, "Be of good cheer! It is I; do not be afraid." Then He went up into the boat to them, and the wind ceased. And they were greatly amazed in themselves beyond measure, and marveled. For they had not understood about the loaves, because their heart was hardened. (Mark 6:49–52 NKJV)

Despite the teaching and miracles that the disciples had already experienced, what was their response after seeing Jesus walk on water?

Though Matthew and John also recount the story of Jesus walking on water, Mark is the only Gospel author to inform us that the disciples did not understand who Jesus was, even after the miracles of feeding the five thousand and walking on the sea. Why was this important to Mark?

If even the disciples, who were with Jesus, failed to recognize the identity and purpose of Christ, how much more diligent must we be in opening our hearts to Him?

JESUS HEALS THE SICK (MARK 6:53–56)

In verses 53–56, we see Jesus at the height of His popularity in the region of Galilee. Crowds of people, likely larger than ever, ran to Him begging only to touch the hem of His garment.

What happened to those who were able to touch Jesus' clothing?

How does this scene contrast with events soon to come?

THE SOURCE OF DEFILEMENT (MARK 7:1–23)

Even in the face of Jesus' many miracles and healings, the Pharisees and scribes strove to find fault with Him.

Read Mark 7:1–13, then answer the following questions.

What was the complaint of the Pharisees and scribes?

What was Jesus' initial response to their criticism?

What did Jesus say they valued over the commandment of God?

Fill in the blanks of this parable by Jesus:

> "Hear Me, everyone, and _____: There is noth-
> ing that _____ a man from outside which
> can _____ him; but the things which come
> _____ of him, those are the things that _____
> a man. If anyone has _____ to hear, let him
> _____!" (Mark 7:14–16 NKJV)

According to verses 20–23, what is the meaning of this parable?

What are the thirteen things that come out of a man and defile him?

1.

2.

3.

4.

5.

6.

7.

8.

9.

10.

11.

12.

13.

Man's Tradition versus God's Law

The Jewish people observed hundreds of traditions passed down from generation to generation that were designed to ensure obedience to God and His Law. Among these was the ceremonial washing of hands with a handful of water, a ritual that was required before every meal. It was especially vital after a trip to the marketplace, where a Jew might come into contact with unclean items such as money or utensils—or even a Gentile!

Over time, these traditions had become so intermixed with Scripture that they were considered as binding as the Law of Moses. Jesus said, however, that a man is not defiled morally by what he eats even if his hands are not ceremoniously washed. He charged the Pharisees and scribes with distorting the Old Testament and focusing on outward conduct rather than the intent of the Law. They had abandoned the commands of God in favor of the traditions of men.

Miracles among the Gentiles
(Mark 7:24–8:10)

Mark now shows Jesus taking His ministry beyond Palestine, apparently for the only time. He traveled to the mostly pagan territory of Tyre, Sidon, and the confederation of cities known as Decapolis. This was a journey of many miles and days, though we have no record of exactly how long this excursion lasted.

One important purpose of the trek was for Jesus to have relatively uninterrupted time to teach the disciples, which had been nearly impossible in Galilee. Three miracles are recorded for us from the time of this journey.

1. Healing a Gentile Woman's Daughter
(Mark 7:24–30)

Jesus entered a house and directed that no one reveal His presence, but a Greek woman with a demon-possessed daughter found out and came to Him.

Read this section, then answer the following questions.

What did Jesus say in response to the woman's request that He cast out the demon in her daughter?

Many scholars interpret Jesus' answer to mean that the children represent His disciples, the children's bread represents His ministry, and dogs represent the Gentiles. What was He really saying to the woman?

What was her respectful reply?

Because of her humility and faith, Jesus granted her request. How might this be an example for our own petitions to the Lord?

2. HEALING A DEAF-MUTE (MARK 7:31–36)

Jesus traveled to the east side of the Sea of Galilee, where people again learned of His presence. They brought Him a man who was deaf and mute, and begged for His healing touch.

Read this section, then answer the following questions.

What did Jesus do as He healed the deaf-mute?

Scholars have speculated that Jesus' sigh in verse 34 is a reflection of compassion for the man or His emotional reaction to battling satanic powers. What do you think?

How is this healing symbolic of Jesus' earthly mission?

3. FEEDING THE FOUR THOUSAND (MARK 8:1–10)

While in the Decapolis region, Jesus and the disciples were again surrounded by a large crowd. As in the incident recorded in Mark 6:32–44, Jesus felt compassion for the people and wished to feed them.

Read this section, then answer the questions below.

How is this account similar to the feeding of the five thousand?

How is it different?

Even though they had "been here before," the disciples didn't seem to see the solution to feeding the multitude. What is Mark telling us about the current condition of the disciples' faith and hearts?

The Pharisees Seek a Sign (Mark 8:11–12)

At Dalmanutha, Pharisees arrived on the scene and began arguing with Jesus, asking for a sign to prove His authority. Everything about their manner and actions indicated that they had already closed their minds to the possibility that Jesus was a messenger of God.

Jesus responded to their questions this way: "But He sighed deeply in His spirit, and said, 'Why does this generation seek a sign? Assuredly, I say to you, no sign shall be given to this generation'" (Mark 8:12 NKJV).

Why did Jesus refuse the Pharisees' request?

When Jesus referred to "this generation," was He speaking only of the Pharisees? To whom else might He have been referring?

The Leaven of the Pharisees and Herod (Mark 8:13–21)

Read Mark 8:13–21, then answer the questions below.

The disciples misunderstood Jesus' words (v. 15). What did they think He was talking about?

What was Jesus really telling them?

A small quantity of leaven, or yeast, can ferment (or infect) a large quantity of bread dough. What does the leaven in Jesus' statement represent?

Jesus asked the disciples a series of nine questions designed to reveal their spiritual dullness. What truth had they missed, not only in this latest incident with the Pharisees but also throughout their time with Jesus?

JESUS HEALS A BLIND MAN (MARK 8:22–26)

We read the account of another healing in Mark 8:22–26. This story is unique among Jesus' miracles, however, in that Jesus laid hands on the man twice.

Read this section, then answer the questions below.

What exactly did Jesus do to restore the blind man's sight?

How might this healing illustrate the disciples own inability to "see" Jesus for who He truly is?

If this is a metaphor, why is it a hopeful one?

Peter Confesses Jesus as the Christ (Mark 8:27–30)

This next section is the turning point in Mark's Gospel. Jesus had progressively revealed His true nature and mission to the disciples, though they had often been slow to grasp His teaching. Now Jesus believed they were ready to understand. He confronted them with a direct question.

Fill in the blanks below, then answer the questions that follow.

> *Now Jesus and His _____ went out to the towns of Caesarea Philippi; and on the road He _____ His disciples, saying to them, "Who do _____ say that I am?" So they answered, "_____; but some say, _____; and others, one of the _____." He said to them, "But who do _____ say that I am?" Peter answered and said to Him, "You are the _____." Then He strictly warned them that they should tell _____ about Him. (Mark 8:27–30 NKJV)*

What three possibilities did people suggest as Jesus' identity?

1.

2.

3.

Whom did Peter correctly identify Jesus as?

THE CHRIST

Christ is a translation of the Greek word *christos*, which means "anointed." The Hebrew translation of the word *messiah* also means "anointed one." One of the meanings of *anoint* is "to choose by divine election." The disciples, then, were finally acknowledging Jesus as God's chosen messenger, the "anointed one."

Jesus rarely used the title *Christ*, however. Of the seven times it appears in Mark, only three are among the saying of Jesus, and only once did He use the title in reference to Himself (9:41). The popular thinking among the Jewish people was that the Messiah would be a powerful ruler bringing political and economic success to God's people and freeing them from Roman domination. Even at the time of Peter's confession, the disciples still held to this view. Yet Jesus' purpose was far different, and much greater, than what they imagined.

PULLING IT ALL TOGETHER . . .

• Jesus gave new authority to His disciples and sent them out to preach on His behalf for the first time.

• John the Baptist was killed, foreshadowing the fate awaiting the Messiah.

• Jesus performed more miracles, which increased His popularity among the people and continued to amaze the disciples. The Pharisees, however, were another matter. They found fault with Jesus, leading to His rebuke of them and the manmade traditions they held so dear.

• On a journey beyond Galilee, Jesus spent more time teaching the disciples and gradually revealing His true nature, partly through more miracles. In another confrontation with

Pharisees, Jesus refused their request for further proof of His divine authority.

• Because the disciples also failed to recognize Him for who He truly was, Jesus asked them a series of pointed questions designed to lead them to the truth.

• Jesus helped a blind man see in what seems a metaphor for His work with the disciples.

• Finally, when asked directly, Peter correctly confessed that Jesus was the Christ, though the disciples still did not realize that their Messiah was not exactly what they expected.

5 JOURNEY TO JERUSALEM

MARK 8:31–10:52

Before We Begin ...

If you were asked to summarize what it means to be a disciple of Jesus, what would you say?

Beginning with this section of his Gospel, Mark shows Jesus moving past the point of leading His disciples to discovering His identity. Jesus now focused on revealing His mission, as well as the implications of that mission for the disciples and all of humanity.

This section is structured around three predictions about Jesus' death and resurrection. Each prediction is followed by a response of the disciples and at least one lesson from Jesus in what it means for them. The setting is the journey by Jesus and the disciples from Caesarea Philippi, some twenty-five miles north of the Sea of Galilee, to Jerusalem, more than sixty miles to the south of the same sea.

FIRST PREDICTION OF DEATH AND RESURRECTION (MARK 8:31–33)

Now that the disciples understood who Jesus was, He immediately began teaching them about the rejection and suffering He would endure, His death, and His resurrection. He no longer spoke in ambiguous parables but talked plainly about what was to come, leading to this exchange with Peter: "Then Peter took Him aside and began to rebuke Him. But when He had turned around and looked at His disciples, He rebuked Peter, saying, 'Get behind Me, Satan! For you are not mindful of the things of God, but the things of men'" (Mark 8:32–33 NKJV).

Why did Jesus refer to Himself as the "Son of Man" (v. 31)?

THE SON OF MAN

Jesus refers to Himself as the "Son of Man" eighty-one times in the Gospels, more than any other title. No one but Jesus used this reference. It appears in the Bible for the first time in Daniel 7:13–14, where the Son of Man is portrayed as a heavenly figure who in the end times is bestowed by God with authority, glory, and sovereign power.

The title is especially appropriate, as it is free of political connotations and will not lead to false expectations. In addition, its meaning is somewhat veiled, preserving the delicate balance between concealment and disclosure that Jesus maintained throughout His earthly mission.

By employing this title immediately after Peter identified Jesus as the Christ, Jesus (and Mark) showed that the "Son of Man" was His own designation for His role as Messiah.

Why did Peter react the way He did to Jesus' prediction of suffering and death?

How did Jesus explain that Satan was behind this response?

THE MEANING OF DISCIPLESHIP (MARK 8:34–9:1)

Jesus began spelling out, both to the disciples and others present, exactly what it means to follow Him.

Fill in the blanks in the passage below, then answer the questions that follow.

When He had called the people to _____, with His disciples also, He said to them, "Whoever desires to come after Me, let him _____ himself, and take up his _____, and _____ Me. For whoever desires to _____ his life will lose it, but whoever _____ his life for My sake and the gospel's will _____ it. For what will it profit a man if he gains the whole _____, and loses his own _____? Or what will a man give in _____ for his soul? For whoever is _____ of Me and My words in this adulterous and sinful generation, of him the _____ also will be ashamed when He comes in the _____ of His Father with the holy angels." And He said to them, "Assuredly, I say to you that there are some standing here who will not taste _____ till they see the kingdom of God _____ with power." (Mark 8:34–9:1 NKJV)

What is the first step required for following Jesus? What does this mean?

What is the second step? Does this mean we must be crucified just as Jesus was?

How can someone lose his life to save it?

What answer fits both of Jesus' questions in verses 36–37?

What did Jesus mean by His use of the word "ashamed"?

What hopeful message did Jesus end this teaching with?

THE TRANSFIGURATION (MARK 9:2–13)

Jesus took Peter, James, and John up to a high mountain, where He changed into another, more glorious form. Elijah and Moses also appeared miraculously, and then God Himself spoke.

Read Mark 9:2–13, then answer the following questions.

How does Mark describe the transfigured Jesus?

What did Peter, in his fear, say?

By equating Jesus, Elijah, and Moses in his suggestion, how did Peter show He still didn't fully understand Jesus' place as the Son of God?

What did God say to them?

What does this mean?

According to Jesus, what had to take place before the three disciples could speak of this event?

Scholars believe that Jesus was referring to John the Baptist when He said, "Elijah has also come" (Mark 9:13 NKJV). How does this fulfill Old Testament prophecy (see Mal. 4:5–6)?

JESUS HEALS A BOY (MARK 9:14–29)

When the three disciples, with Jesus, returned from the incredible spiritual experience on the mountain, they were confronted with the cold reality of a seemingly difficult, earthly problem. A man explained that his son was possessed by a spirit. He had brought his son to the other disciples and asked for help, but they had been unable to cast out the demon.

Read Mark 9:14–20, then answer the following questions.

What did Jesus say when He learned that the disciples had been unable to cast out the demon?

What was the primary obstacle preventing the disciples from success?

What did the boy, possessed by the spirit, do when he saw Jesus?

Jesus asked the father how long the boy had been possessed. The father replied:

> *"From childhood. And often he has thrown him both into the fire and into the water to destroy him. But if You can do anything, have compassion on us and help us." Jesus said to him, "If you can believe, all things are possible to him who believes." Immediately the father of the child cried out and said with tears, "Lord, I believe; help my unbelief!" (Mark 9:21–24 NKJV)*

Based on the father's testimony, what was the demon's intent?

How do we know that the father's faith in Jesus was shaken by the disciples' lack of success?

What did Jesus say to the father? How is this statement a summary of what Jesus had been trying to teach throughout His ministry?

How does the father's answer represent the spiritual status of the disciples—and indeed, so many believers today?

Read Mark 9:25–29, then answer the questions below.

What did the disciples ask Jesus when they were alone?

How would prayer have changed the disciples' ability to cast out the demon?

SECOND PREDICTION OF DEATH AND RESURRECTION (MARK 9:30–32)

Once again, Jesus foretold of His betrayal, death, and resurrection, and once again, the disciples failed to understand—or refused to accept—His words.

Read Mark 9:30–32, then answer the following questions.

Who did Jesus say would kill him?

Why might the disciples have been afraid to ask Jesus what He meant?

WHO IS THE GREATEST? (MARK 9:33–37)

Jesus and the disciples returned to Capernaum. On the way, the disciples argued about who among them would be the greatest in the coming kingdom. Jesus used the opportunity to teach them another aspect of discipleship.

Fill in the blanks below, then answer the questions that follow.

> And He sat down, called the _____, and said to them, "If anyone desires to be _____, he shall be last of all and _____ of all." Then He took a little _____ and set him in the midst of them. And when He had taken him in His _____, He said to them, "Whoever _____ one of these little children in My name receives _____; and whoever receives Me, receives not Me but _____ who sent Me." (Mark 9:35–37 NKJV)

What was Jesus saying here concerning the importance of earthly status?

How important is an attitude of service to God?

What and whom did the little boy represent in this lesson?

How did Jesus stress the significance of giving attention and kindness even to little children?

JESUS FORBIDS SECTARIANISM (MARK 9:38–42)

In Mark 9:38–42, Jesus learned that the disciples had stopped a man who had been driving out demons in His name. Jesus responded:

> *"Do not forbid him, for no one who works a miracle in My name can soon afterward speak evil of Me. For he who is not against us is on our side. For whoever gives you a cup of water to drink in My name, because you belong to Christ, assuredly, I say to you, he will by no means lose his reward.*
>
> *"But whoever causes one of these little ones who believe in Me to stumble, it would be better for him if a millstone were hung around his neck, and he were thrown into the sea." (Mark 9:39–42 NKJV)*

Why would the disciples have chosen to stop this man?

What reward was Jesus talking about in verse 41?

What are the implications of Jesus' inclusive attitude for the divisions among believers and churches today?

What will happen to anyone who discourages others from believing in Jesus?

SIN AND DISCIPLESHIP (MARK 9:43–50)

Read Mark 9:43–50, a commentary by Jesus on sin and the demands of discipleship, then answer the following questions.

Did Jesus mean that a sinner should literally cut off his hand or foot? What was His point?

What did He mean by "enter into life" (vv. 43, 45 NKJV)?

Many interpretations have been suggested for the meaning of verse 49, including that everyone who enters hell will suffer its fire or that every Christian in this life will undergo the fire of suffering and purification. What is your interpretation?

Pure salt was an invaluable preservative in the ancient world, while impure salt could deteriorate and easily become worthless. What did Jesus mean when He commanded the disciples, "Have salt in yourselves" (v. 50 NKJV)?

How does Jesus' final instruction—"Have peace with one another"—relate to His earlier comments about arguments over status in the kingdom?

Marriage and Divorce (Mark 10:1–12)

In Judea, Jesus again taught and preached to large crowds. And again the Pharisees came to test Him, this time asking whether it was lawful for a man to divorce his wife. Jesus pointed them to the Old Testament, asking what Moses commanded, and the Pharisees replied that Moses permitted a man to write a certificate of divorce.

Fill in the blanks of Jesus' response below, then answer the questions that follow.

And Jesus answered and said to them, "Because of the _____ of your _____ he wrote you this precept. But from the _____ of the creation, God 'made them _____ and _____.' 'For this reason a man shall _____ his father and mother and be _____ to his wife, and the two shall become _____'; so then they are no longer _____, but one flesh. Therefore what God has joined _____, let not man separate." (Mark 10:5–9 NKJV)

GROUNDS FOR DIVORCE

Under the Law of Moses, a man could divorce his wife when he found "some uncleanness in her" (Deut. 24:1 NKJV). The Jews were divided about what this meant. Some followed the strict view of Rabbi Shammai, which allowed divorce only if a wife was guilty of adultery; others favored the more lenient view of Rabbi Hillel, which allowed a husband to divorce his wife for almost any reason, even for burning a meal.

Divorce required a certificate, a public document granting a woman the right to remarry without civil or religious sanction. Women were not allowed to initiate divorce under Jewish law. A Roman woman, however, could legally divorce her husband.

In His statements to the Pharisees and disciples, Jesus showed that the intent of the Law of Moses was to discourage divorce under any circumstances. Though His comments recorded in the Gospel of Matthew seemed to leave open the possibility of divorce in the case of adultery (Matt. 5:32; 19:9), Jesus clearly indicated that marriage should be viewed as a covenant of mutual fidelity. It is to be a lifelong union under the headship of God.

How did the Pharisees hope to trap Jesus with their question about divorce?

Why, according to Jesus, did Moses permit divorce?

Where does God stand on the issue of divorce?

Read Mark 10:10–12, then answer the questions below.

What clarification did Jesus add regarding the matter of divorce?

Why is verse 12 significant for Mark's Roman readers?

JESUS BLESSES LITTLE CHILDREN (MARK 10:13–16)

Mark 10:13–16 shows Jesus' affection for little children and the need for childlike trust and faith among believers.

Read these verses, then answer the following questions.

Why did the disciples rebuke those who brought children to Jesus?

What did Jesus mean by "of such is the kingdom of God" (v. 14 NKJV)?

How can a helpless child be better suited to receive the gift of eternal life than an adult?

THE FOLLY OF TRUSTING IN RICHES (MARK 10:17–31)

Jesus encountered a rich man on the road who asked what he had to do to inherit eternal life.

Read Mark 10:17–22, then answer the following questions.

In verse 18, Jesus was not denying His deity but attempting to move the man's focus away from what was good or not good. Why did He do this?

How successful had the man been in keeping the commandments listed by Jesus?

What was the "one thing" he lacked according to Jesus?

What did the rich man do when Jesus told him he must sell his possessions?

Is this required of everyone who would follow Jesus? If not, why did Jesus require it of this man?

Jesus used the conversation with the rich man to deliver another lesson to the disciples. He said to them:

> "How hard it is for those who have riches to enter the kingdom of God!" And the disciples were astonished at His words. But Jesus answered again and said to them, "Children, how hard it is for those who trust in riches to enter the kingdom of God! It is easier for a camel to go through the eye of a needle than for a rich man to enter the kingdom of God." (Mark 10:23–25 NKJV)

The disciples were surprised at Jesus' words because they considered wealth a sign of God's favor. How can riches be an obstacle to entering God's kingdom?

Why did Jesus refer to the disciples as children (v. 24)?

Jesus referred to the rewards that await those who follow Him in Mark 10:26–30. Read these verses, then answer the following questions.

Why were the disciples overwhelmed (v. 26)?

Why is understanding Jesus' answer in verse 27 so critical to accepting the gift of salvation?

What does Jesus promise to those who leave house or brothers or sisters or father or mother or wife or children or lands for His sake?

Verse 31 seems to be a summary of Jesus' teaching about the servant nature of discipleship. Why is this so appropriate as a conclusion to this section?

THIRD PREDICTION OF DEATH AND RESURRECTION (MARK 10:32–34)

On the road to Jerusalem, Jesus made His third and most explicit prediction of His betrayal, death, and resurrection. The disciples were astonished at His determination to press on.

Read Mark 10:32–34, then answer the questions below.

Who would the Son of Man be betrayed to?

Who would He then be delivered to?

What four things would the Gentiles do to Jesus before He rose again?

1.

2.

3.

4.

GREATNESS IS SERVING (MARK 10:35–45)

In a remarkable parallel to the discussion in Mark 9:33–37, Jesus again dealt with the presumptuous ambition of a small group of His disciples, in this case James and John, the sons of Zebedee. Once again, after revealing the terrible and wonderful fate awaiting Him, Jesus had to turn His disciples' thoughts from status to service.

Read Mark 10:35–45, then answer the following questions.

What did James and John ask of Jesus?

Why did Jesus say He couldn't grant their request?

What was the reaction of the other disciples when they heard of the request?

What did Jesus say was His mission on earth (v. 45)?

A WORD FOR REDEMPTION

When Mark quotes Jesus as saying the Son of Man came to "give His life a ransom for many" (Mark 10:45 NKJV), the word "ransom" comes from the Greek *lytron*, literally translated "price of release." Jesus' death was a payment for sin that would set people free—an act of redemption. *Lytron* is used only one other time in the New Testament, in Matthew 20:28.

Other New Testament Words for Redemption

Greek Word	English Meanings	References
agorazo (verb)	to buy, to purchase in the market (or slave market)	1 Corinthians 6:20; 7:23; 2 Peter 2:1; Revelation 5:9; 14:3–4
apolytrosis (noun)	a buying back, a setting free by paying a ransom price	Luke 21:28; Romans 3:24; 8:23; 1 Corinthians 1:30; Ephesians 1:7, 14; 4:30; Colossians 1:14; Hebrews 9:15; 11:35
exagorazo (verb)	to buy out, to purchase out of the market (or slave market)	Galatians 3:13; 4:5; Ephesians 5:16; Colossians 4:5
lytroomai (verb)	to ransom, to free by paying a ransom price	Luke 24:21; Titus 2:14; 1 Peter 1:18
lytrosis (noun)	an act of freeing by paying a ransom price	Luke 1:68; 2:38; Hebrews 9:12

Jesus Heals Blind Bartimaeus (Mark 10:46–52)

Mark records one last miracle healing as an example and conclusion to his discussion about discipleship. It shows that in
spite of the disciples' inability to understand, through their
faith Jesus would open their eyes so they would finally see and
comprehend who He was and what His purpose was on earth.

Read Mark 10:46–52, then answer the questions below.

*By addressing Jesus as "Son of David," what understanding did
Bartimaeus show about the identity of Jesus?*

*What can we learn today from the persistence Bartimaeus dis-
played in seeking Jesus?*

*Despite Jesus' determined movement toward Jerusalem, what
did He do when He realized the need of Bartimaeus?*

*What key element did Bartimaeus provide that led to his heal-
ing?*

What did Bartimaeus do when he received his sight?

PULLING IT ALL TOGETHER . . .

• Jesus began teaching His disciples openly about His betrayal, death, and resurrection. Upon hearing this, Peter rebuked Jesus and was rebuked in turn for what seems a Satan-inspired effort to distract Jesus from His mission.

• Jesus also began teaching more plainly about what it means to follow Him. The disciples learned that "whoever desires to save his life will lose it, but whoever loses his life for My sake and the gospel's will save it" (Mark 8:35 NKJV).

• Peter, James, and John accompanied Jesus to a high point on a mountain, where they saw Jesus transfigured, witnessed the miraculous appearance of Elijah and Moses, and heard the voice of God. They were told to say nothing of what they had seen until Jesus had risen from the dead.

• Jesus made two more predictions about His betrayal, death, and resurrection. He taught the disciples many lessons about a servant attitude, sectarianism, sin and discipleship, marriage and divorce, childlike trust, wealth, and salvation.

• The disciples failed to absorb many of Jesus' lessons, twice initiating discussions centering on their status in the future kingdom.

• Jesus healed a faithful blind man, teaching the disciples that through their faith, He would open their eyes so they would finally see and comprehend who He was and what His purpose was on earth.

6 JERUSALEM MINISTRY

MARK 11:1–13:37

Before We Begin . . .

As you look at the world today, do you feel we are in the end times? Why or why not?

The next three chapters of the Gospel of Mark focus on Jesus' ministry in Jerusalem. Jesus' entry into Jerusalem during the Passover celebration marked the beginning of Passion Week and the events leading to the fulfillment of His purpose on earth. Mark records His triumphal entrance into the city as well as His symbolic judgment on a fig tree and His clearing of the temple courts.

Later, Mark chronicles five conflicts with Jewish leaders at the temple. He concludes this section with Jesus' prophetic Olivet Discourse, as it is now known, to the disciples on the Mount of Olives.

Read Mark 11:1–8, then answer the following questions.

What did Jesus command two of the disciples to do?

An unused animal was often regarded as especially suitable for religious purposes. How did Jesus describe the colt the disciples were to find?

Fill in the blanks of this passage describing the excited shouts of the people as Jesus rode into the city, then answer the questions that follow.

"_____!

'_____ is He who comes in the name of the _____!'

Blessed is the _____ of our father _____

That comes in the _____ of the Lord!

Hosanna in the _____!"

(Mark 11:9–10 NKJV)

After so often keeping His presence a secret, why did Jesus now enter Jerusalem in a way that called great attention to Himself?

"Hosanna" was considered an enthusiastic welcome to pilgrims or a famous rabbi. Did the people understand that Jesus was the Messiah?

SIGNS OF JUDGMENT ON ISRAEL (MARK 11:12–26)

The following passages are packaged in a "sandwich" structure that Mark often employs in his Gospel. We read of Jesus' initial encounter with a fig tree, followed by the story of the clearing of the temple, followed by a return to the fig tree and a lesson on faith and forgiveness from Jesus.

Read Mark 11:12–14, then answer the following questions.

What did Jesus say to the fruitless fig tree?

Many scholars believe that the fig tree in this story represents the people of Israel. If this is so, what was Jesus saying about spiritually barren people?

After reaching Jerusalem, Jesus was outraged at what He saw when He entered the temple. He drove out those who had turned the area into a market and flipped over the tables of the moneychangers and the benches of those selling doves. Then He taught the people: "Is it not written, 'My house shall be called a house of prayer for all nations'? But you have made it a 'den of thieves'" (Mark 11:17 NKJV).

Read Mark 11:15–19, then answer the questions below.

What caused Jesus' indignation at the temple?

Why did He say the people had made it a den of thieves?

WORSHIPING AT THE TEMPLE

The Law of Moses commanded worship and sacrifice to be celebrated at a central sanctuary, a place chosen by God (Deut. 12:5–7). This place was generally identified as Jerusalem, and one hundred thousand people or more would travel to the city for Passover.

Those who came to the temple for Passover needed to buy lambs for slaughter. Doves were required for the purification of women (Lev. 12:6; Luke 2:22–24) and the cleansing of people with certain skin diseases (Lev. 14:22). Doves were also the customary offering of the poor (Lev. 5:7). In order to make these purchases and to fulfill offerings and taxes, the people depended on moneychangers to turn their foreign coins into the local currency.

The temple itself was divided into separate sections of worship for the Jews and the Gentiles. The large outer court of the Gentiles was the only place they were allowed to worship and pray—but as Jesus saw, it was also where the moneychangers had set up shop, along with sellers of items and animals needed for temple sacrifice. What so incensed Jesus was that these activities (some no doubt involving profitable markups for the moneychangers and sellers) were being performed in a holy place and were distracting those who had come to worship.

Some people today view Jesus only as a passive and gentle Savior, incapable of strong emotion and action. How are Jesus' deeds at the temple at odds with this view?

Once again, Jesus' bold actions drew attention to Himself. What was the response of the scribes and chief priests?

Why did they want to kill Jesus?

Read about Jesus' lessons on faith and forgiveness in Mark 11:20–26, then answer the following questions.

Peter was apparently surprised to see the ruined fig tree. What do the fig tree and Jesus' words about casting mountains into the sea indicate about the power of faith?

What did Jesus say in verse 24?

Though not stated here, what is the other implied requirement of receiving whatever is prayed for (see Matt. 6:9–10; 1 John 5:14–15)?

Notice Jesus' comments in verses 25–26. What was He saying about the link between effective prayer and forgiveness?

What happens if we fail to forgive?

CONFLICT WITH JEWISH RELIGIOUS LEADERS (MARK 11:27–12:37)

The next section of the book of Mark deals with Jesus' conflicts with the Jewish religious leadership in Jerusalem, which was showing increasing hostility toward Him. Mark portrays the contrast between self-righteous religion and wholehearted devotion to God. Five incidents are recounted here, all within the area of the temple.

1. JESUS' AUTHORITY QUESTIONED (MARK 11:27–12:12)

Representatives of the Sanhedrin challenged Jesus as He walked into the temple, asking who gave Him authority to purge the temple. Jesus responded with a question of His own: "I also will ask you one question; then answer Me, and I will tell you by what authority I do these things: The baptism of John—was it from heaven or from men? Answer Me" (Mark 11:29–30 NKJV).

Read Mark 11:27–33, then answer the questions below.

By His question, Jesus implied that both John's ministry and His own were sanctioned by God. Why would answering, "Heaven," place the religious leaders in an awkward position?

Why, taking into account the widespread belief among the people that both John and Jesus were prophets of God, would answering, "Men," be equally awkward for the priests, scribes, and elders?

What did the religious leaders say in an attempt to save face?

What did Jesus say in return?

Jesus then related a parable about wicked vinedressers to the religious leaders. Read the parable in Mark 12:1–9, then answer the questions below.

Who does the vineyard owner represent in the parable?

Who are the wicked vinedressers?

Whom do the servants represent?

Who is the beloved son of the vineyard owner?

What warning was Jesus giving the religious leaders? How was it also a prediction?

Fill in the blanks below, then read verse 12 and answer the questions that follow.

> *"The stone which the builders _____*
>
> *Has become the chief _____.*
>
> *This was the _____ doing,*
>
> *And it is _____ in our eyes."*
>
> *(Mark 12:10–11 NKJV)*

What is the meaning of this quote from Psalm 118?

What was the response of the religious leaders?

2. PAYING TAXES TO CAESAR (MARK 12:13–17)

In an effort to trick Jesus into a phrase they could use against Him, a group of Pharisees and Herodians offered false compliments to Jesus and asked whether it was lawful in God's view to pay taxes to Caesar.

To Pay or Not to Pay

An annual and highly unpopular poll tax had been required of all Jews by the Roman emperor since AD 6, when Judea became a Roman province. Funds went directly into the emperor's treasury. Some Jews flatly refused to pay it, believing that payment was an admission of Roman right to rule.

The Pharisees were also against the tax but were willing to use its existence to test Jesus with a religious question. The Herodians, on the other hand, supported foreign rule and agreed with the tax. They were most concerned about the political implications of Jesus' answer to their question. The intent of both groups was to entrap Him. If Jesus supported paying the tax, He would antagonize the people and discredit His claim as God's messenger. But to openly oppose the tax invited retaliation and persecution from Rome.

The tax payments were made with denarii, coins that bore the image of Caesar and inscriptions that read "Tiberius Caesar Augustus, Son of the Divine Augustus" on one side and "Chief Priest" on the other. The claim to the divinity of Caesar originated out of the imperial cult of emperor worship and particularly offended the Jews.

Read about the discussion on taxes between the Pharisees and Herodians and Jesus, then answer the following questions.

How did Jesus show that He knew the true intent of His questioners?

How did Jesus acknowledge Caesar's earthly authority and appear—at first—to give one of the answers the Pharisees and Herodians were looking for?

How did Jesus then show that Caesar's authority went only so far?

3. SADDUCEES AND THE RESURRECTION (MARK 12:18–27)

The next opponent to confront Jesus was a group of Sadducees, members of a Jewish party representing the wealthy and sophisticated classes. The Sadducees denied the resurrection, rejected oral tradition, and accepted only the five books of Moses as authoritative.

Read this section, then answer the questions below.

How did the Sadducees appear to ridicule the concept of resurrection with their fabricated story about one wife and seven brothers?

How did Jesus show that the Sadducees' question was irrelevant (v. 25)?

In verse 26, quoting from Exodus 3:1–6, how did Jesus show that God is a God of the living?

4. THE FIRST COMMANDMENT OF ALL (MARK 12:28–34)

A scribe, probably a Pharisee, had been listening to Jesus' conversation with the Sadducees and was impressed by Jesus' answers. Traditional Mosaic Law contained 613 individual commandments—365 negative and 248 positive. The scribe, apparently with no hidden motives, asked Jesus which of all these was the most important commandment. Jesus replied:

> "The first of all the commandments is: 'Hear, O Israel, the LORD our God, the LORD is one. And you shall love the LORD your God with all your heart, with all your soul, with all your mind, and with all your strength.' This is the first commandment. And the second, like it, is this: 'You shall love your neighbor as yourself.' There is no other commandment greater than these." (Mark 12:29–31 NKJV)

Why do you think Jesus introduced the first commandment with the Shema, a Jewish confession of faith recited by devout Jews every morning and evening?

What is the key element of the first of all commandments?

What are the four ways Jesus commands us to love God?

1.

2.

3.

4.

Why did Jesus put such emphasis on linking "Love your neighbor as yourself" to the first commandment?

How can these two commandments be seen as a summary of everything stated in the Law and the Prophets?

Read the final exchange between the scribe and Jesus in Mark 12:32–34, then answer the following questions.

In his response to Jesus, what bold insight did the scribe offer in verse 33?

How did Jesus respond to the scribe?

Why did the Pharisees and others give up their questioning?

5. SON OF DAVID, LORD OF DAVID (MARK 12:35–37)

Read this section, which covers Jesus' teaching about the common Jewish belief that the Messiah would be a descendant of David, and answer the following questions.

Why did Jesus quote from Psalm 110 and point out David's reference to "my Lord," that is, the Messiah?

Jesus seemed to imply that the Messiah was both David's descendent and David's Lord—both human and divine. Though the common people in the crowd delighted in His teaching, do you think they understood His meaning?

For those who understood—and undoubtedly at least some of the Pharisees and scribes did—Jesus was making a veiled claim to His own status as the Messiah. Why would He add this claim to an already tense situation?

BEWARE OF THE SCRIBES (MARK 12:38–44)

In the final account of His public ministry in the Gospel of Mark, Jesus denounced the hypocrisy of the scribes. It was a bold challenge to the Pharisees and others of the same mind, furthering their determination to dispose of Him at any cost. Making His statement even more pointed, Jesus contrasted their ostentatious conduct with a widow's small but wholehearted gift to God.

Read Mark 12:38–44, then answer the following questions.

In what six ways did Jesus say the scribes showed their hypocrisy?

1.

2.

3.

4.

5.

6.

Who would condemn them for their conduct?

When the poor widow gave two mites (worth a fraction of a penny) as a freewill offering at the temple, how much money did she keep for herself?

How is it that the widow gave more than anyone else?

What lesson was Jesus teaching the disciples about wholehearted commitment to God?

THE DESTRUCTION OF THE TEMPLE
(MARK 13:1–13)

Chapter 13, known as the Olivet Discourse because it was delivered by Jesus on the Mount of Olives just outside of Jerusalem, includes two specific predictions of future events. In both cases, Jesus warned of terrible moments to come.

The first focus was on the near future—the destruction of Jerusalem by the Roman army (which came to pass in AD 70). The second focus was on the far future and the events surrounding the end of time, which will include the return of the Son of Man in His glory.

Read the first thirteen verses of chapter 13, then fill in the blanks of Jesus' statement below and answer the questions that follow.

> "Take heed that no one _____ you. For many will come in My _____, saying, 'I am _____,' and will deceive many. But when you hear of _____ and rumors of wars, do not be _____; for such things must _____, but the _____ is not yet. For _____ will rise against nation, and _____ against kingdom. And there will be _____ in various places, and there will be _____ and _____. These are the beginnings of _____." (Mark 13:5–8 NKJV)

How did Jesus answer a disciple's admiring comment about stones and buildings? What was He foretelling?

What are the signs of the "beginnings of sorrows" that are not to be viewed as the end of the age?

Are we in the "beginnings of sorrows" today?

What suffering and persecution did Jesus predict for the disciples?

Must we as believers also be prepared for suffering and persecution for His sake?

What hope and help did Jesus offer the disciples—and by implication, all believers?

THE GREAT TRIBULATION (MARK 13:14–23)

Jesus then spoke to the second question of the disciples: "What will be the sign when all these things will be fulfilled?" (Mark 13:4 NKJV).

Read Mark 13:14–23, then answer the questions that follow.

THE SIGN OF ABOMINATION

The primary sign for the Jews at the end times will be an "abomination" that leads to desolation, first mentioned in Scripture in the book of Daniel (see Dan. 9:25–27). The word "abomination" denoted pagan idolatry and its practices, while "abomination of desolation" referred to the presence of an idolatrous person or object so abhorrent that it caused the temple to be abandoned.

The first fulfillment of Daniel's prophecy was the desecration of the temple in 167 BC by Syrian ruler Antiochus Epiphanes. Later writings, such as 1 Maccabees and the Psalms of Solomon, use Daniel's terms to describe the continued attacks on Jerusalem's temple. Not all scholars today believe that this abomination will be repeated in the future, but most agree that at least part of it has already taken place.

Some scholars say that Jesus' words in Mark 13:14–23 refer only to the chaotic years before Jerusalem's fall in AD 70. Others believe they apply only to the Great Tribulation to come. Still others suggest that Jesus was talking about *both* events—that the destruction of Jerusalem was a foreshadowing of the terrible events due at the end of the age. In the latter two viewpoints, the abomination "standing where it ought not" (Mark 13:14 NKJV) is believed to be the Antichrist, an end-times figure who will make a covenant with the Jewish people, then break it, desecrate the temple, and declare himself God.

Why did Jesus place such emphasis on the urgency of flight (vv. 14–18)?

How did Jesus describe the coming tribulation (v. 19)?

What warning did Jesus give (vv. 22–23)?

THE COMING OF THE SON OF MAN (MARK 13:24–37)

Jesus then described what will be His dramatic return after the times of trouble, an appearance that will involve all the skies and the heavens:

> *"The sun will be darkened, and the moon will not give its light; the stars of heaven will fall, and the powers in the heavens will be shaken. Then they will see the Son of Man coming in the clouds with great power and glory. And then He will send His angels, and gather together His elect from the four winds, from the farthest part of earth to the farthest part of heaven." (Mark 13:24–27 NKJV)*

What will be the unmistakable signs of the coming of the Son of Man?

Who are the "elect"?

Read Mark 13:28–37, then answer the questions below.

What is the meaning of the parable of the fig tree?

TRIBULATION THEORY

You may have heard your more theologically inclined Christian friends debate the merits of Pretribulation and Posttribulation theory. *Pretribulation* refers to the idea that Jesus will come for the church, the body of Christ, at the beginning of the tribulation period. This will include believers from that time as well as those who have already died. Both will be "raptured," that is, swept up with Jesus to receive their resurrected bodies (see 1 Thess. 4:17). Believers past and present will be spared from the agony of God's final judgment on the earth.

Though many Christians adhere to Pretribulation theology, some prefer the *Posttribulation* viewpoint. This means the "elect" will include the redeemed of all ages—past, present, and future. The body of Christ will remain on earth throughout the tribulation period and be supernaturally protected. These believers will then be raptured at the end of the Great Tribulation.

Modern scholars continue to deliberate over both of these viewpoints and many variations of them. The study of the end times is known as *eschatology*.

A "generation" can mean one's contemporaries or a group of people descended from a common ancestor. What do you think Jesus meant by His use of this word in verse 30?

The disciples asked about specific signs so they would recognize the coming of the end times. But what did Jesus say about the day and hour of His return?

How does this add a sense of urgency to our spiritual lives?

PULLING IT ALL TOGETHER . . .

• Jesus rode a donkey into Jerusalem amid the shouts and cheers of a Jewish population gathering to celebrate Passover.

• While in Jerusalem, Jesus cleared the temple of money-changers and marketers and caused a fig tree to wither, apparently a warning of judgment to come.

• During five incidents in the temple, Jesus rebutted challenges from members of the Sanhedrin and taught lessons on His authority and ancestry as the Messiah, payment of taxes, the resurrection, and the commandments. His responses and teaching only increased the determination of the Jewish leadership to kill Him.

• On the Mount of Olives, Jesus spoke to the disciples of incredible events to come—the destruction of Jerusalem, the Great Tribulation at the end of the age, and the return of the Son of Man in glory.

7 | SUFFERING AND DEATH

MARK 14:1–15:47

Before We Begin . . .

If you had been a follower of Jesus at the time of His arrest and crucifixion, do you think you would have stood by Him in His final hours?

Chapters 14 and 15 of the Gospel of Mark detail Jesus' betrayal, arrest, trials, and death by crucifixion. They also complete themes introduced earlier in the book of Mark, including Jesus as the Messiah, Jesus' conflicts with the Jewish religious leaders, the disciples' failure to understand Jesus' true identity and purpose, and the ultimate act of service—Jesus' sacrifice as a "ransom for many."

The first part of this section of Mark's Gospel relates Jesus' betrayal by one of His disciples, the Passover meal known as the Last Supper, and the disciples' desertion of Jesus.

Read Mark 14:1–9, then answer the questions below.

What did the woman do with the flask of costly oil (v. 3)?

How did those nearby react?

Fill in the blanks of Jesus' response:

> "Let her alone. Why do you _____ her? She has done a _____ work for Me. For you have the _____ with you always, and whenever you _____ you may do them _____; but _____ you do not have always. She has _____ what she could. She has come beforehand to _____ My body for _____. Assuredly, I say to you, wherever this _____ is preached in the whole _____, what this woman has _____ will also be told as a _____ to her." (Mark 14:6–9 NKJV)

Read Mark 14:10–11 about Judas's betrayal, then answer the following questions.

The priests and scribes of the Sanhedrin had planned to wait until after the eight-day festival, when the crowds had dispersed, to seize Jesus (v. 2). Why did their timetable change?

Which single motive or combination of motives suggested for Judas's betrayal of Jesus seems most likely to you?

1. Judas responded to the official call for Jesus' arrest (see John 11:57).

2. Judas was disillusioned because Jesus had failed to establish the kind of earthly kingdom he expected.

3. Judas's greed got the best of him.

4. Judas gave in to Satan's whispers (see Luke 22:3; John 13:2, 27).

THE LORD'S SUPPER (MARK 14:12–26)

Jesus gathered the disciples for the Passover meal in the Upper Room and announced that one of the Twelve would betray Him.

Read Mark 14:12–21, then answer the questions below.

Why was Jesus so secretive about the location of the Upper Room?

How did Jesus' words "who eats with Me" heighten Judas's treachery?

How did the disciples react to Jesus' announcement that one of them was a betrayer?

Though Jesus' betrayal and death were already "written," do you think Judas acted of his own will in becoming the instrument of that terrible destiny?

We learn from the Gospel of John (John 13:30) that Judas left the room after taking the bread. Then Jesus began the events instituting what we know today as the Lord's Supper:

> *And as they were eating, Jesus took bread, blessed and broke it, and gave it to them and said, "Take, eat; this is My body." Then He took the cup, and when He had given thanks He gave it to them, and they all drank from it. And He said to them, "This is My blood of the new covenant, which is shed for many. Assuredly, I say to you, I will no longer drink of the fruit of the vine until that day when I drink it new in the kingdom of God."*
> *(Mark 14:22–25 NKJV)*

A NEW COVENANT

According to Jewish tradition, before eating the Passover meal, the head of the house would explain the meaning of each of the elements as it related to Israel's deliverance from slavery in Egypt. For the bread, for example, he would say, "This is the bread of affliction which our ancestors ate when they came from the land of Egypt."

In the Upper Room, Jesus reinterpreted the elements of the Passover meal in light of a new covenant. The bread represented His physical body, soon to be broken; the wine, His blood, soon to be shed. By this new covenant, Jesus' death on the cross substituted for the sins of humankind. Through our faith in Jesus, we can now achieve the spiritual blessings Israel expected God to grant in the last days. The physical blessings God promised Israel, however, will not be fulfilled until the second coming of Christ.

Today, partaking of the Lord's Supper is a common and significant act of worship for Christians at churches around the world.

How was Jesus both looking back and looking ahead as He introduced the new covenant?

What day was Jesus referring to in the phrase "that day when I drink it new in the kingdom of God"?

JESUS PREDICTS PETER'S DENIAL (MARK 14:27–31)

Read about Jesus' prediction of Peter's denial in Mark 14:26–31, then answer the questions below.

In Jesus' words, why would the disciples be made to "stumble"?

Who was so sure of his faith and courage that he promised to die with Jesus rather than deny Him?

Why did Peter think Jesus was wrong about him? Who ended up being right? What does this say about our own self-assuredness in the face of God's Word?

GETHSEMANE (MARK 14:32–52)

Jesus' prayer at Gethsemane, a gardenlike enclosure in an olive orchard, is one of the most powerful moments in Scripture. The full weight of what was about to take place seemed almost to overwhelm Jesus. Alone except for three disciples who failed in their duty to keep watch, Jesus was distressed and grieved nearly to the point of dying. Never was He more like us, more human—yet never did He provide a better example of obedience to the will of God.

Read Mark 14:32–42, then answer the questions below.

What did Jesus say to Peter, James, and John after becoming deeply distressed?

Jesus uses the term "Abba," an intimate expression for "father," in His prayer to God (v. 36). It is the only time this word appears in the Gospels. Why would Mark include this detail at this moment?

In His humanity, what did Jesus ask for (v. 36)?

As a loving Son, how did He qualify His request? How are His words a model for our own prayers?

What did Jesus say to the disciples in verse 38? What does this indicate about the presence of Satan?

Judas, knowing that Gethsemane was a favorite meeting place of Jesus and the disciples, arrived with a band armed with swords and clubs, sent by the Sanhedrin.

Read Mark 14:43–52, then answer the following questions.

How did Judas identify Jesus to the multitude?

How did one disciple resist Jesus' arrest? According to John 18:10, who was this disciple?

What did Jesus say in protest to His captors?

What is the meaning of His words "But the Scriptures must be fulfilled" (Mark 14:49 NKJV)?

What happened to the disciples? Why doesn't Mark simply say, "The disciples fled"?

Verses 51–52, about the young man who followed Jesus, then fled just as the disciples did, emphasize the point that Jesus' supporters had abandoned Him; He was utterly alone. Many scholars believe that in this passage, unique to the Gospel of Mark, the young man is Mark himself. It was common practice at the time for an anonymous writer to insert a brief personal story as an author "signature."

Who were the "young men" who grabbed on to Mark (if he was indeed the fleeing man)?

JESUS FACES THE SANHEDRIN (MARK 14:53–65)

After His arrest, Jesus faced two trials, the first by the religious authorities and the second by the political leadership. The Sanhedrin had the authority to arrest Jesus but not to execute him.

Read Mark 14:53–59, then answer the questions below.

Who was the lone disciple with the courage to follow Jesus, albeit at a distance?

What false charges were made against Jesus?

What difficulty did the Sanhedrin face in convicting Jesus (vv. 56, 59)?

Fill in the blanks of this exchange between the high priest and Jesus in verses 60–62, then read though verse 65 and answer the questions that follow.

> And the _____ stood up in the midst and asked _____, saying, "Do You _____ nothing? What is it these men _____ against You?" But He kept _____ and answered nothing. Again the high priest asked Him, saying to Him, "Are You the _____, the Son of the _____?" Jesus said, "_____. And you will see the _____ sitting at the right hand of the _____, and coming with the clouds of _____." (Mark 14:60–62 NKJV)

What was Jesus' response to the high priest's questions (v. 60)?

Why did Jesus declare publicly for the first time that He was the Son of God (v. 62)?

After the members of the Sanhedrin sentenced Jesus to death for blasphemy, how did they show their contempt for Him?

PETER DENIES JESUS (MARK 14:66–72)

Read about the three accusations against Peter in the courtyard at the end of chapter 14, then answer the questions below.

Who accused Peter of being a disciple of Jesus? How did Peter respond?

Peter's denial was so strong that the third time he was accused of being one of the disciples, he swore he wasn't (in a legal sense, not as profanity). Why was he so emphatic?

What did Peter do after hearing the rooster crow?

JESUS FACES PONTIUS PILATE (MARK 15:1–15)

On Friday morning of Passion Week, after sentencing by the Sanhedrin, Jesus appeared before Pontius Pilate, the Roman governor or prefect of Judea. This time, Jesus faced political charges.

Read the first five verses of chapter 15 and answer the following questions.

How did Jesus respond to Pilate's question about His kingship?

How did Jesus answer other charges?

What are the similarities between Jesus' appearance before Pilate and His appearance before the Sanhedrin?

The next section highlights the complete rejection of Jesus by all of humanity. We see in verse 10 that Pilate knew Jesus was innocent of charges by the religious authorities. Yet the people, given the chance to spare God on earth, cried for Him to be put to death. There was no answer to Pilate's question, "What evil has He done?" but bloodlust. The religious authorities, the political authorities, and the common people all took an active role in unjustly condemning Jesus.

Read Mark 15:6–15 and answer the questions below.

As prefect, Pilate had the power to free Jesus at any moment he chose. How does his failed attempt at arranging an expedient excuse for releasing Him represent our sometimes feeble efforts to do the will of God?

How does Jesus' taking on the sentence originally reserved for Barabbas symbolize His sacrifice for all of humanity?

THE MOCKERY OF JESUS (MARK 15:16–20)

Mark describes in great detail the indignities suffered by Jesus at the hands of the people and the Roman soldiers. Read verses 16–20, then list six specific ways the soldiers mocked Jesus.

1.

2.

3.

4.

5.

6.

THE CRUCIFIXION (MARK 15:21–41)

Mark is restrained in describing Jesus' actual death on the cross. Jesus had already been scourged, which means He was beaten on the back with a leather whip that had bone, rock, or metal affixed to its ends. He had also been forced to carry the crossbeam for His crucifixion, probably weighing about one hundred pounds, to the knoll called Golgotha. We learn that He was so weak that soldiers compelled a bystander, Simon, to help carry the crossbeam.

Mark's Roman readers would have well understood the gruesome details of the crucifixion itself. Customarily, a condemned man was stripped naked, except perhaps for a loincloth, and stretched out on the ground. Both forearms were nailed to the crossbeam. This beam was then raised and fastened to an upright post, and the victim's feet were nailed to the post. A painful death usually followed sometime during the next two or three days.

Read Mark's account of the crucifixion of Jesus in verses 21–37, then answer the questions below.

In what ways did the people continue to mock Jesus even as He was dying on the cross?

When Jesus cried out, "My God, why have You forsaken Me?" do you think it was His human side expressing anguish, His divine side lamenting separation from God, or perhaps some combination of both?

Jesus' loud cry just before death indicates He was conscious when He died, unlike most victims of crucifixion. Why do you think it happened this way?

KING OF THE JEWS

The official reason for Jesus' execution at the hands of the Romans was treason against the state, since Jesus affirmed Pilate's question about His claim to kingship. Though Pilate did not believe that Jesus was a true king, he ordered the title "King of the Jews" to be posted on the cross, perhaps as a warning to Jewish aspirations of independence.

It was Roman custom to write the name of a man condemned to crucifixion and a summary of his crime on a board and affix it to his cross. All four Gospels include the text of Jesus' notice, though each varies slightly, probably because it was recorded in three languages. Mark's version is the most concise. Neither Pilate nor his men nor the crowd of people on hand understood how accurate these words actually were.

Fill in the blanks describing the response to the death of Jesus, then answer the questions below.

Then the veil of the _____ was torn in two from top to bottom. So when the _____, who stood opposite Him, saw that He _____ out like this and _____ His last, he said, "Truly this _____ was the Son of _____!" (Mark 15:38–39 NKJV)

Only God could have torn the curtain inside the temple at this exact moment. What was the meaning of this supernatural act?

How is the centurion's declaration a fitting confirmation of Jesus' identity as the Son of God?

THE BURIAL OF JESUS (MARK 15:42–47)

Read Mark 15:40–47 regarding the witnesses to Jesus' final moments on the cross and His burial, then answer the questions below.

Why did Joseph of Arimathea, a member of the Sanhedrin, risk public condemnation by asking for the body of Jesus?

According to Mark, what two women witnessed both Jesus' final breath and His laying in the tomb?

PULLING IT ALL TOGETHER . . .

- The members of the Sanhedrin looked for a way to arrest and kill Jesus without stirring up the crowds of people in Jerusalem. One of the disciples, Judas Iscariot, provided the opportunity they were looking for when he offered to hand over Jesus.

- At their Passover meal, Jesus revealed to the Twelve that one of them would betray Him. He instituted what is now known as the Lord's Supper, telling the disciples that the bread represented His physical body and the wine represented His blood. On the Mount of Olives, Jesus told the disciples that each of them would fall away, though Peter claimed otherwise.

• At Gethsemane, Jesus was overtaken with sorrow and distress. He prayed for God to remove the burden He was about to bear—but then submitted Himself to His Father's will, providing a prayer model for all believers to follow. Judas arrived with an armed band sent by the Sanhedrin, and Jesus was arrested. Though Peter initially resisted, cutting off the ear of one man, everyone soon deserted Jesus.

• Jesus was put on trial before the Sanhedrin. At first He refused to respond to the false charges against Him, but when asked, He openly declared that He was the Son of Man, God's Son. The members of the Sanhedrin condemned Him to death and mocked and beat Him.

• In the courtyard, Peter denied three times that he was a disciple of Jesus. A rooster crowed twice, reminding Peter of Jesus' words, and he became deeply grieved.

• Jesus came before Pilate the next morning and confirmed that He was King of the Jews, though He did not answer to any other charges. Pilate went before a crowd and offered to release either Jesus or a prisoner named Barabbas. The crowd called for Barabbas to be released and Jesus to be crucified.

• Roman soldiers mocked Jesus, scourged Him, and forced Him to carry a crossbeam to Golgotha. There Jesus was crucified. The people continued to taunt Jesus as He died. Darkness fell over the land. Jesus cried out, "My God, why have You forsaken Me?" After a last loud cry, Jesus died. Joseph of Arimathea, a member of the Sanhedrin, asked for Jesus' body and buried Him in a tomb cut from rock. A stone was rolled against the entrance, supposedly putting an end to the remarkable ministry of the Nazarene named Jesus.

RESURRECTION

MARK 16:1–20

Before We Begin . . .

What was the most surprising or shocking event of your life? Do you think it would match the surprise that awaited the three women at Jesus' tomb after His crucifixion?

In just a few paragraphs, Mark describes the events that changed the course of history and brought hope to all of humanity. These events began with three women, two of whom witnessed the death and burial of Jesus, returning to the tomb with plans to anoint the body of Jesus. Instead of a body, however, they found a young man dressed in white, believed by most Bible interpreters to be an angel. The angel said to them, "Do not be alarmed. You seek Jesus of Nazareth, who was crucified. He is risen! He is not here. See the place where they laid Him. But go, tell His disciples—and Peter—that He is going before you into Galilee; there you will see Him, as He said to you" (Mark 16:6–7 NKJV).

Read Mark 16:1–8, then answer the questions below.

Since Sunday is considered the first day of the week, how many days had passed since the burial of Jesus?

What practical concern did the women have before their arrival at the tomb?

Was the angel singling out Peter or indicating that he was forgiven for his denials and still considered a disciple?

How did the women respond to the appearance and words of the angel?

WHOSE ENDING IS THIS?

The Gospel of Mark ends on a note of some historical controversy, as authorship of the final twelve verses is questioned by scholars as much as any other passage in the New Testament. One of the reasons is that some early manuscripts do not include this ending and stop at verse 8, while others support the inclusion of verses 9–20. One tenth-century manuscript attributes the final verses to a contemporary of the early church bishop Papias (AD 60–130).

An examination of the text itself also raises questions about authorship. The transition from verse 8 to 9 is abrupt and introduces Jesus only as "He"; the vivid style of the rest of the Gospel is gone; and many of the Greek words in the final verses do not appear elsewhere in the Gospel or are used in a different manner.

Because of these issues, scholars have suggested a variety of possible reasons why the Gospel might actually have ended at verse 8, including the following: (1) Mark's original ending was lost or destroyed. (2) Mark's original ending was removed for an unknown reason. (3) Mark was unable to complete his Gospel, possibly because of his death. And (4) Mark intended to end his Gospel at verse 8. No one today knows for certain.

Even if another Christian writer penned these final twelve verses sometime around the end of the first century, they combine elements of post-resurrection appearances found in the other three Gospels and are considered historically accurate by scholars.

Three Appearances (Mark 16:9–14)

Three appearances by the risen Jesus are recorded here—one to Mary Magdalene, one to two of the disciples as they traveled to Emmaus, and one to all eleven of the disciples.

Read Mark 16:9–14, then answer the following questions.

To whom does the risen Jesus first appear?

How did the disciples respond to her incredible news?

How did the rest of the disciples respond to the report by two of them that they too had seen Jesus?

What did Jesus say to the still-disbelieving disciples (v. 14)?

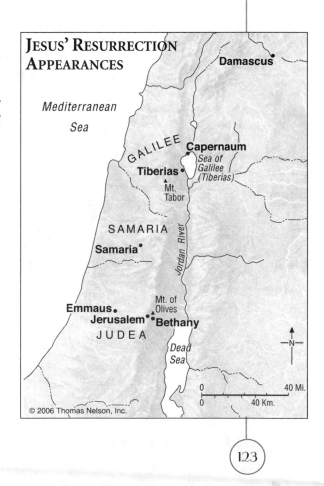

Jesus' Resurrection Appearances

Damascus

Mediterranean Sea

GALILEE

Capernaum
Sea of Galilee (Tiberias)

Tiberias

Mt. Tabor

SAMARIA

Samaria

Jordan River

Emmaus

Jerusalem

Bethany

Mt. of Olives

JUDEA

Dead Sea

0   40 Mi.
0   40 Km.

—N—

© 2006 Thomas Nelson, Inc.

THE EYES AND EARS OF MARY MAGDALENE

We have already seen that Mary Magdalene was among the women who witnessed the death of Jesus on the cross. All four Gospels also agree that Mary was in the group that first arrived at the empty tomb. And both Mark and Matthew record the appearance of the risen Jesus to Mary Magdalene; she was most likely the first person to see the resurrected Christ.

What is interesting about all this is that the testimony of a woman had no legal value in Jewish society at the time. Had early church writers wanted to fabricate a story about resurrection, it's highly unlikely they would have chosen a woman to corroborate it. The repeated inclusion of Mary Magdalene's testimony in the Gospels is just one more sign of their authenticity.

THE GREAT COMMISSION (MARK 16:15–18)

Fill in the blanks of Jesus' missionary commission to the disciples and description of signs to believers, then answer the questions that follow:

"Go into all the _____ and preach the gospel to _____ creature. He who _____ and is baptized will be _____; but he who does not believe will be _____. And these _____ will follow those who believe: In My name they will _____ demons; they will speak with new _____; they will take up _____; and if they _____ anything deadly, it will by no means hurt them; they will lay _____ on the sick, and they will _____." (Mark 16:15–18 NKJV)

How did Jesus summarize the disciples' mission from this day forward?

Though Jesus mentioned baptism as an outward display of faith, what did He indicate is the one requirement for salvation?

What are the signs for believers mentioned by Jesus?

THE ASCENSION OF JESUS (MARK 16:19–20)

The last two verses of the Gospel of Mark emphasize in one sense the completion of Jesus' ministry on earth and in another sense the beginning of the spreading of His message through His disciples. Jesus' authority was affirmed as He took His rightful place at the right hand of God. Yet even as Jesus assumed His residence in heaven, He started working through the disciples—and by implication, continues to work through all believers today—to proclaim the gospel to every corner of the world.

The Gospel of Mark concludes with these words:

> *So then, after the Lord had spoken to them, He was received up into heaven, and sat down at the right hand of God. And they went out and preached everywhere, the Lord working with them and confirming the word through the accompanying signs. Amen. (Mark 16:19–20 NKJV)*

PULLING IT ALL TOGETHER . . .

• Mary Magdalene, Mary the mother of James, and Salome went to Jesus' tomb on Sunday morning hoping to anoint His body. Instead, however, they were met by an angel who told them that the crucified Jesus was risen. They were instructed to tell the disciples and Peter.

• Jesus made three post-resurrection appearances—to Mary Magdalene, to a pair of the disciples, and then to the gathered disciples. He rebuked them for their unwillingness to believe the eyewitness testimony of their fellow believers.

• Jesus proclaimed the missionary commission of the disciples and described signs that would accompany those who believe.

• His time on earth complete, Jesus ascended into heaven and assumed His rightful place at the right hand of God. The disciples began spreading the gospel message, with Jesus working through them and authenticating their efforts with signs of the Word of God.

9

COMING TO A CLOSE

More than any other Gospel and perhaps more than any other book in the Bible, the Gospel of Mark puts us "on the scene" for the incredible events of his narrative. In his vivid and breathless style, Mark allows us to experience the ministry, miracles, death, and resurrection of Jesus of Nazareth, the Son of God, as if we were in Galilee and Judea ourselves. Message, theology, and historical record notwithstanding, perhaps the chief value of the book of Mark is its ability to roll away the centuries, allowing us to meet and travel with Jesus during His amazing final days on earth.

As we have seen, Mark puts great emphasis on the works of Jesus. We observe repeated miracles—casting out demons, healing blind men, feeding multitudes with only a small quantity of bread and fish—that clearly demonstrate His divinity. Yet we also discover that as the Messiah, Jesus had come not to rule (as the disciples and Jewish people expected), but to serve. He would give His own life so that all of us have the chance to be forgiven of sin and gain eternal life.

In the disciples, we most likely see ourselves. Frequently fearful and slow to understand Jesus' messages, identity, and purpose, they failed Jesus completely at the hour He needed them most. The impetuous and audacious Peter, considered Mark's chief eyewitness source for the events in his Gospel, failed most spectacularly of all. He denied Jesus three times after promising, "If I have to die with You, I will not deny You!" (Mark 14:31 NKJV).

Yet this same group of "underachieving" disciples gives us great hope. Peter was forgiven, and by finally relying completely on Jesus, the disciples discovered the faith and courage to establish the early Christian church. Most died a martyr's death for the cause of spreading the message of Christ throughout the world.

We certainly understand the humanity of the disciples—we witness their flaws as well as their successes. Perhaps more compelling in Mark, however, is that we also see the human side of Jesus. He had compassion for the hungry crowds of people who had come to hear Him teach (Mark 6:34). He was indignant at seeing the temple of God defiled (Mark 11:15–17). He was so distressed over the terrible events and separation from God to come that He asked His Father to take away this responsibility (Mark 14:35–36).

These are emotions we can identify with. Jesus lived as we live and suffered as many of us suffer. One of the great achievements of Mark's Gospel is that we gain an intimate picture of the sacrifice Jesus made to become one of us. This is service and love in its highest form. It fills in the significance of the words of Jesus as He summarized His mission on earth: "The Son of Man did not come to be served, but to serve, and to give His life a ransom for many" (Mark 10:45 NKJV).

How to Build Your Reference Library

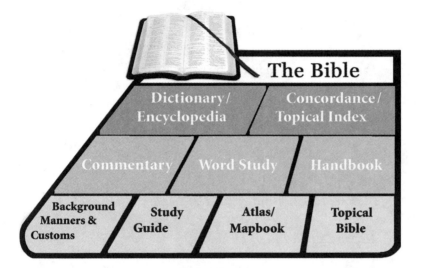

The Bible

Dictionary/Encyclopedia

Concordance/Topical Index

Commentary

Word Study

Handbook

Background Manners & Customs

Study Guide

Atlas/Mapbook

Topical Bible

GREAT RESOURCES FOR BUILDING YOUR REFERENCE LIBRARY

DICTIONARIES AND ENCYCLOPEDIAS

All About the Bible: The Ultimate A-to-Z® Illustrated Guide to the Key People, Places, and Things

Every Man in the Bible by Larry Richards

Every Woman in the Bible by Larry Richards and Sue Richards

Nelson's Compact Bible Dictionary

Nelson's Illustrated Encyclopedia of the Bible

Nelson's New Illustrated Bible Dictionary

Nelson's Student Bible Dictionary

So That's What It Means! The Ultimate A-to-Z Resource by Don Campbell, Wendell Johnston, John Walvoord, and John Witmer

Vine's Complete Expository Dictionary of Old and New Testament Words by W. E. Vine and Merrill F. Unger

CONCORDANCES AND TOPICAL INDEXES

Nelson's Quick Reference Bible Concordance by Ronald F. Youngblood

The New Strong's Exhaustive Concordance of the Bible by James Strong

COMMENTARIES

Believer's Bible Commentary by William MacDonald

Matthew Henry's Concise Commentary on the Whole Bible by Matthew Henry

The MacArthur Bible Commentary by John MacArthur

Nelson's New Illustrated Bible Commentary

Thru the Bible series by J. Vernon McGee

HANDBOOKS

Nelson's Compact Bible Handbook

Nelson's Complete Book of Bible Maps and Charts

Nelson's Illustrated Bible Handbook

Nelson's New Illustrated Bible Manners and Customs by Howard F. Vos

With the Word: The Chapter-by-Chapter Bible Handbook by Warren W. Wiersbe

For more great resources, please visit *www.thomasnelson.com.*

NELSON IMPACT™ STUDY GUIDES

NELSON IMPACT
A Division of Thomas Nelson Publishers
Since 1798

www.thomasnelson.com